POWER OF ATTORNEY

Other books by Mark Stevens:

LAND RUSH
THE BIG EIGHT
THE ACCOUNTING WARS
MODEL

POWER OF ATTORNEY:
The Rise of the Giant Law Firms

by Mark Stevens

McGraw-Hill Book Company
New York   St. Louis   San Francisco
Toronto   Hamburg   Mexico

1 2 3 4 5 6 7 8 9 D O C D O C 8 7 6

ISBN 0-07-061290-0

LIBRARY OF CONGRESS CATALOGING-IN-PUBLICATION DATA

Stevens, Mark, 1947–
  Power of attorney.
  Includes index.
    1. Law partnership—United States.   2. Law firms—
United States.   3. Practice of law—United States.
I. Title.
KF300.S72   1986   346.73′0682   86-10494
ISBN 0-07-061290-0   347.306682

Book designed by: Mark Bergeron

To Harly David,
THE ONE AND ONLY

Contents

Preface

In writing about the nation's "giant" law firms, an author is faced with an immediate problem: how to define "giant." Is the key criterion the number of lawyers? Gross annual fees? Number of offices? Or are measures of profitability, such as net profits or profits per partner, more meaningful? Surprisingly, firms that are substantial in one or more of these categories are lightweights in others. Take New York's Wachtell, Lipton, Rosen & Katz, regarded by many as the premier merger and acquisition practice in the nation. Measured by profits per partner, it tops the list of all law firms, but Wachtell is a relative lilliputian in number of lawyers. Conversely, Baker & McKenzie, the largest law firm when ranked by number of lawyers, is a distant runner-up in profits per partner. And so it goes throughout the rankings.

If size has no standard measurement, how about power? This too is an amorphous criterion. How will power be gauged? In winning landmark cases? In attracting major clients? In bringing change to the legal profession? While Milbank, Tweed, Hadley & McCloy is a power in the banking industry, its influence on the changing complexion of major law firms is almost nil. And though Finley, Kumble, Wagner, Heine, Underberg, Manley & Casey is rarely associated with legal scholarship, it has been a catalyst for change (though its competitors are loath to admit this) in the legal profession.

With no single criterion emerging as a reliable indicator of the firms' impact and influence on the profession, I consider the giant firms those that have more than 300 lawyers and meet at least one of the following additional tests:

- Leadership in the move toward multicity practice
- Strong growth record
- Innovation in marketing and other business disciplines

From among the twenty or so firms that could qualify for "giant" status, I have further narrowed coverage in this book via an entirely qualitative criterion: I have covered those firms that due to the nature of their practice, their internal politics, or their influence behind closed doors are fascinating creatures whose machinations reveal something important about the law and the lawyers and law firms in the top echelons of the legal profession.

POWER OF ATTORNEY

1

Breaking the Speed Limit: Milbank, Tweed and the Megafirms

"Managing a major law firm is like leading the opera with 75 prima donnas trying to sing at once."

Alexander Forger, chairman, Milbank, Tweed, Hadley & McCloy

On a raw winter morning in early February 1985, Alexander Forger, chairman of Wall Street's venerable Milbank, Tweed, Hadley & McCloy, addressed a gathering of associates to make a rather surprising announcement. Stodgy, time-warped Milbank—best known as the lawyers to New York's Chase Manhattan Bank for as long as anyone could remember—would be exploring a series of unprecedented actions that for this staunch defender of the legal status quo would be positively revolutionary. In effect, Milbank would be joining the more aggressive players among the nation's prominent law firms.

A tall, angular gentleman with a lined, leathery face and bushy walrus eyebrows that make him look older than his 62 years, Forger had risen to the firm's top spot only seven months before, capping a 35-year career as an estate and matrimonial lawyer to such illustrious clients as Jacqueline Onassis and Joan Kennedy. As he stood before the associates, dressed in a hand-tailored gray flannel suit, crisply starched white shirt, and royal blue cravat, Forger clearly relished his

1

role as a visionary leader prompting a hidebound institution to awaken to the demands of the late 20th century. The class of '50 Yalie knew full well that the young lawyers in attendance, all of whom aspired to Milbank partnership and some of whose lives would be inexorably bound up with the firm for the next half century, would appreciate his message.

It was, after all, a message of confidence, of energy, of a legal institution often handcuffed by the past now repositioning itself for continued prosperity and, although no one was admitting it, for its long-term survival. A belated start, perhaps, but only recently had the need for change become clear to Milbank's leaders. New forces at work in the legal marketplace made it imperative.

Standing before the Milbank lawyers, Forger outlined his action plan:

> **STEP ONE:**   Expand Milbank's scope of practice beyond the traditional banking services that have long buttered the bread of Wall Street lawyers. (Diversifying, the firm would create in-house practice boutiques similar to those of uptown Manhattan rival Skadden, Arps, Slate, Meagher & Flom, easily the most successful law firm of the decade.)
>
> **STEP TWO:**   Establish a West Coast beachhead through a merger with a well-connected Los Angeles firm, possibly bringing as many as 100 new lawyers into the Milbank fold.
>
> **STEP THREE:**   Create the new position of "senior associate" for those lawyers passed over for partnership but willing and able to play a continuing role with the firm.
>
> **STEP FOUR:**   Reward star associates with substantial year-end bonuses.

While the enrapt associates (surprised as much that they were being informed of the plan as they were of the plan itself) were pleased by Forger's comments, the partners were less than unanimous in their support. In the days that followed, critical, often embarrassing questions arose inside Milbank and throughout the legal grapevine. Had the partners been informed of Forger's plans before they were revealed to the associates? Were they in agreement with his near- and long-term objectives? Did they share his vision of the new Milbank?

One observer familiar with Milbank's internal machinations reports that news of the chairman's remarks started a political brouhaha behind the firm's closed doors.

"Forger believed in what he had to say, and for good reason. He'd put together a balanced plan for addressing some of the problems of a legal dowager that had been trying to bury its head to changes in the profession. If he could be faulted, it's that he got a bit carried away by his own enthusiasm and made it sound as if he was running faster than Milbank's internal speed limit allowed.

"Soon after he addressed the associates, one of the youngsters leaked his plans to the *American Lawyer*, which ran an article, 'Milbank Tells Associates All,' playing up the prospect of an LA merger. While expansion to the West Coast had been approved by the partnership in principle, nothing—as far as any of the partners knew— was imminent, and few had contemplated merging with a firm anywhere near as big as 100 lawyers. Some of the old boys in the firm were more than a bit upset by that prospect, which they made abundantly clear to Forger. Faced with this rumbling in the ranks, he decided—and wisely so—to modify his statements without accepting or denying the accuracy of the news reports."

Questioned about the merger proposal soon after the story appeared, Forger gave what appeared to be a stay-up-all-night-thinking-of-the-right-response response. This time he was staying well within the Milbank speed limit.

"Sometimes the press takes things out of context. I never told the associates we'd merge with a 100-lawyer firm. My statement, which came in response to an associate's question about mergers, was that we'd talk to any size firm, even one with as many as 80 or 100 lawyers. But I never said we would proceed with such a deal, and I hasten to add that a merger of that magnitude is highly unlikely in my lifetime."

Clearly, Forger found himself between a rock and a hard place. His master plan to breathe new life into Milbank, Tweed was designed not to put his personal stamp on the firm, but instead as a direct response to a gathering threat in the upper echelons of legal practice: the rise of the giant law firms. A threat that, regardless of Milbank's internal politics, would not simply vanish in thin air.

Some relatively new, some with pedigrees dating back as far as Milbank's, the giant firms are distinguished by huge, mostly national

practices that are outstripping their competitors in scope of legal services, cultivation of new markets, staff size, fees, and in some cases
profits. Drawing their strength from a rich lode of clients and/or a
cohesive strategy for practice expansion (some say "domination"),
they are a menace to every major law firm in the nation.

Among the giant firms* are:

- Baker & McKenzie (home office Chicago)
- Sidley & Austin (Chicago)
- Finley, Kumble, Wagner, Heine, Underberg, Manley & Casey (New York)
- Fulbright & Jaworski (Houston)
- Morgan, Lewis, Bockius (Philadelphia)
- Skadden, Arps, Slate, Meagher & Flom (New York)
- Gibson, Dunn & Crutcher (Los Angeles)
- Weil, Gotshal & Manges (New York)
- Shearman & Sterling (New York)
- Jones, Day, Reavis & Pogue (Cleveland)
- Pillsbury, Madison & Sutro (San Francisco)
- O'Melveny & Myers (Los Angeles)

The legal giants have experienced explosive growth in the past decade,
turning what were relatively small firms as late as the 1970s into
professional behemoths virtually overnight. In the process they have
given rise to a new class of law firm—one with a voracious appetite
for growth and a built-in capacity to expand, often at the expense of
smaller competitors.

In its 1984 survey of the nation's top 500 law firms, the *Legal
Times* noted that

> The rich get richer, they say—or at least among the nation's large
> law firms, the big get bigger. . . . Firms in this year's top 200 did

---

*Some firms (such as New York's Cravath, Swaine & Moore), though smaller
in numbers of lawyers than the megafirms, equal or exceed them in power and wealth,
but this is limited to a select few.

grow in size by an average of 6.8 percent. . . . the 10 largest law firms reported an average increase of 13.2 percent. . . .

Extrapolating from the numbers, the publishers observed that

> We are also seeing firms of a size unprecedented in the profession. New York's Shearman & Sterling has 409 lawyers; in 1970 the firm had 164 attorneys and in 1960 only 106. At Sidley & Austin, another shop of more than 400 lawyers, there were just 79 attorneys in 1970 and 51 in 1960. The large legal enterprise is a reality on today's legal map. The only remaining questions seem to be, will we see a 1,000 lawyer firm before 1990.
>
> Stephen and Lynn Glasser,
Legal Times, September 24, 1984.

The giant law firms are divided into two camps: those relative newcomers that have risen to prominence through marketing prowess, and others that have built on a legacy of blue-chip clients tracing back a century or more. The difference in ancestry makes for a cultural clash akin to John McEnroe taunting the Wimbledon aristocracy. Partners at New York's Shearman & Sterling, a ranking member of the Brahmin camp, consider themselves to be in a different profession than their counterparts at Finley, Kumble. And in a sense they are. The culture at Finley, Kumble is that of a business that happens to be practicing law; Shearman's culture is precisely the opposite, that of a law practice that happens to be in business. While Shearman is trying desperately to preserve its traditions, Finley is too young and irreverent to have or want any. While Shearman is shy about marketing, Finley wrote the book. And while Shearman's growth has come mostly from within, Finley is a veritable patchwork of acquired firms and partners stitched together under a single letterhead.

In the way they respond to changes in the marketplace and the way they have risen to the ranks of the giants, the firms represent two extremes in the modern law profession. One strives for collegiality, the other for competition. Night and day. Black and white. Both are convinced not only that theirs is the enlightened approach, but that the other's is headed down the road to ruin.

To those firms locked in competition with the megafirms, the distinctions that divide them are not as important as the fact that the megafirms, like marauding imperialists, are extending their influence over an ever wider domain of corporate clients. To some they appear unstoppable. But to others it is simply a matter of moving, posthaste, to the law-firm-as-a-business philosophy—to competing with the more aggressive megafirms on an equal footing.

For Alexander Forger and his counterparts among a new wave of managing partners, the need to compete more effectively with the giant firms is clear. But to do so, they must introduce business disciplines to a profession that still prides itself on scholarly pursuits. It is an effort that pits purists against opportunists, partner against partner, firm against firm. Iconoclastic in-house lawyers (also known as corporate counsel) and their allies among the megafirms have challenged and in many cases reversed the status quo that prevailed at the pinnacle of legal practice for generations. In the process, the old white-shoe firms, Milbank among them, have been forced to reevaluate their most sacrosanct practices with an eye toward becoming more effective competitors. As Alexander Forger discovered, the process can be a slow and bloody one.

"The dilemma in managing a law firm today is that you recognize the need to move ahead but you also recognize that in doing so you are letting yourself in for an experience that is infinitely more challenging and exhausting than doing nothing at all," Forger says. "Because once you commit yourself, and in turn your firm, to a certain action, you set in motion a series of events that bruises egos and ruffles feathers. You pay a price for that—my word, you do—but the other side of that coin is that the price for doing nothing is far greater.

"The practice of law has changed dramatically in recent years; it is changing this very moment. To be successful—to survive—you have to change with it."

2

Power Struggle: The Rise of the Corporate Counsel

"Whenever the law firms call up saying they've got some fantastic new way to cut our legal bills, I reach into my back pocket and take a firm grip of my wallet."

Robert Banks, vice president and general counsel, Xerox Corporation

The rise of the giant law firms coincides with a critical change in the way corporate clients view their law firms.

For more than a century the major industrial corporations and money center banks that became the bedrock clients of the biggest and wealthiest law firms were virtual captives of their legal relationships. The leading law firms, which had come to prominence advising the great industrialists and financiers of the late 19th and early 20th centuries, continued to counsel the companies they formed long after the founders passed from the scene. As the corporations expanded and the business environment in which they operated became more complex and litigious, the firms added partners and associates to service their clients' proliferating legal needs.

In time, the lawyers were regarded not as purveyors of a service, but as part of the corporate family and as defenders of its interests. A senior partner would serve on the board of directors and, in the most incestuous relationships, be named corporate counsel, serving as the client's top staff lawyer while remaining a member of its outside law firm.* In this questionable arrangement, rife as it is with potential conflicts of interest, the lawyer responsible for acquiring legal services often passed the work to his own firm and shared in the profits.

But even in less blatant cases, where the corporate counsel had no links to the outside law firm, he rarely functioned as an effective arbiter of the firm's fees and practices. With the real legal power vested outside the corporation (as it had been since the founder's days), the corporate counsel's job was that of a glorified coordinator, handling the administrative housekeeping of the lawyer-client relationship. Discreetly ridiculed by corporate management and outside lawyers alike, the post was widely considered a consolation prize for laggards unable to cut the mustard as law firm partners.

Convinced of their own inferiority and easily intimidated by the firms theoretically under their control, corporate counsel deferred to the outside lawyers. As a result, the law firms went virtually unchallenged in establishing fees, billing terms, and practice standards. They prospered handsomely. Admission to the partnership of a leading firm was a virtual guarantee not only of tenured employment but of a lifetime of steadily increasing earnings unmatched by a lawyer's counterparts in the other learned professions.

In this environment, competition was very much a gentlemanly affair. With the banks and manufacturing corporations pacing America's industrial expansion—and with the Securities Acts and New Deal legislation complicating business transactions—the workload grew faster than the firms' ability to service it. Protected by their captive relationships, the established practices had no reason to fear competitive assaults and were not, in turn, moved to encroach on their competitors' turf. Blessed with virtual monopolies in their respective markets, they focused instead on practice standards, on establishing self-indulgent compensation systems, and on perfecting the mystique and the mannerisms of elite professionals. How cases were staffed and billed, how partners were selected and paid, and how new partners were admitted to the ranks were issues based on internal considerations rather than market factors. Free to conduct their affairs as they saw fit, the estab-

---

*Though less common today, these relationships are still in evidence at a number of major corporations.

lished practices could all but ignore such boorish concerns as efficiency, productivity, marketing, and competition.

Until the tide began to turn. Beginning in the late 1960s and accelerating in the following decades, clients began to reevaluate both the nature of their law firm relationships and their methods of acquiring legal services. With fees soaring both in real terms and as a percentage of corporate overhead—and with domestic corporations facing stiffer competition at home and abroad—management began applying to the former sacred cow, legal services, the same rigorous cost controls it had long applied to other services. History's longest honeymoon was over.

With this change in attitude came a significant upgrading in the position of corporate counsel. If power was to shift in-house, management recognized, it would need a strong and capable legal executive on staff. No longer a go-between for the outside lawyers, the corporate counsel was anointed a senior management officer charged with overall responsibility for the corporation's legal affairs. In this sweeping realignment, the once-omnipotent law firm now reported to the corporate counsel and served entirely at his discretion. Given this infusion of clout and prestige, the post began to attract a higher caliber of attorney, equal in skill, education, and, perhaps most important, self-confidence to his peers in private practice.

The change was dramatic, prompting a top-to-bottom restructuring of the lawyer-client relationship. Unlike their predecessors—mostly meek second-raters hired to accommodate the outside lawyers—the new breed of bold and ambitious corporate counsel was charged with managing them. In the process, they soon recognized that their interests often clashed with the law firms'. In the new scheme of things, the corporate counsel would earn his stripes not by coddling the outside firms, but by reducing their fees, by shifting more and more of the workload in-house, and by severing relationships built on old school ties in favor of those based on legal expertise and sound economics.

The firms responded to this insurrection in one of two ways. Those most accustomed to a sheltered environment (read "monopolistic relationships") stubbornly resisted change and, with a customary arrogance, continued to practice law as they thought it should be practiced—with little or no concern for the clients' economics.

But where the intransigent saw only problems, problems they chose to ignore, those who viewed the legal profession as a business and who were willing to openly admit as much to themselves and to their partners glimpsed an extraordinary opportunity to leapfrog older and more established firms to a prominent, perhaps leading position on corporate legal practice. In a market where talent and productivity are prized over mystique and tradition, they knew that even a newly minted firm could compete head to head with the great legal institutions in New York, Chicago, Los Angeles, and San Francisco.

The tactic was simple yet brilliant: to forge an alliance with the new genus of corporate counsel who, like the upstart firms themselves, had a vested interest in dismantling the old system of hiring, firing, and compensating lawyers. Rather than resist change they would actively pursue it, consciously rewriting the rules of law firm conduct as they applied to internal administration and client relations. Policies and procedures would be based not on the law firm's haughty self-image or on its affection for precious legal traditions, but instead on market factors. In a nutshell, law firm management would change its perspective from an inward to an outward view, adapting to client needs rather than expecting the opposite.

The strategy worked magnificently. New York's Skadden, Arps, Slate, Meagher & Flom—leading practitioners of the new business-minded law—opened its doors in 1948, the year Milbank celebrated its 82nd birthday. Today Skadden, almost double Milbank's size, is regarded as a superb law firm by Milbank's own chairman—one, although he's diplomatic about it, it appears he'd like to emulate.

"While I'm not looking to create a mirror image of Skadden, Arps, there are some lessons to be learned from the way they've achieved such astonishing growth," Forger says. "What impresses me is the planning that's gone into it. They've identified those types of legal services promising the greatest growth and have formed practice units to go out and get the business. That makes more sense than just tacking on groups of lawyers willy-nilly, with no conscious plan of where you are and where you want to go. Skadden has grown within an established framework. I admire that."

But respect has come grudgingly. Quick to dismiss the Skaddens in their midst as crude and commercial purveyors of undignified legal services—such as counsel for proxy battles and property closings—the old-line firms only began to change their prehistoric views in the late seventies. And not by choice. With the hungry practitioners rapidly encroaching on their established markets and with the chilling specter of many once-prominent sister firms suffering drastic declines in gross fees and partner compensation, the new generation of managing partners that replaced the curmudgeons of the past moved to reposition their firms as more effective competitors. But change in an established law firm comes only by rewriting the near-holy rules that define its character. As Forger discovered, this is never easy.

"People who grow up in a successful law firm such as this one, and who stay with it for the course of their careers as our partners are wont to do, tend to be pleased with the status quo and committed to preserving it," Forger says. "Not because they're bad guys or pigheaded or any such easy, black-and-white answer, but because they like the system. They like the compensation, the collegiality, the fine style of practice that has characterized this firm's culture for the century or more since its founding.

"So when someone like myself comes along suggesting some alternative approaches, they retort that this will change the firm's culture and that must not be allowed to happen. But heck, I liked it much better when we were 36 partners and could sit around a table deciding all the issues. That doesn't mean we can turn back the clock. The culture will change if we want it to change or not. Changes in the way clients consume legal services are forcing us to make changes in the way we deliver them. The question is whether we control those changes or let them control us.

"Consider, for example, the evolving needs of our banking clients. In the increasingly volatile world of financial services, banks are moving away from reliance on traditional interest-based lending to investment banking, capital market transactions, and municipal finance. When a bank like Chase Manhattan moves into municipal finance, they want their law firm to help guide them through that expansion. Well, what happens if we don't have a strong municipal finance practice? In the past, a law firm could get by by telling the client, 'We have a bright young partner who's just right for that kind of work. Give us time to train him and he'll be on the job before you know it.' Impossible today. Clients—and rightly so—aren't willing to subsidize these internal training programs. If you're minus a skill they need when they need it, they'll shop the market for a firm that can fill the bill regardless of how long you've been their lawyers.

"To be prepared for our clients' needs before they come knocking at our door, I've suggested that each of our departments identify skills they'd like to add to their practices and that they consider hiring headhunters to go out and find the appropriate people to join us from other firms. Sure, that violates the Milbank tradition of grooming partners in-house, and sure, that may bring a change in our culture, but as I tell my partners, change will come anyway. Should we lose clients, should compensation decline, should this place become a less enjoyable place to practice, the culture will surely suffer.''

Perhaps, but at least some of Forger's 77 partners don't buy the argument. Each of the action steps outlined in his talk to the firm's associates represented a break from tradition that is resisted by factions within the House of Milbank:

- The call to create practice boutiques—popularized by the marketing-oriented megafirms—is based on the recognition that corporate counsel, like Milbank's banking clients, have shifted from reliance on a single firm to a more discriminating policy of shopping the market for specialized services. The corporation anticipating Justice Department objections to a planned merger with an industry competitor, for example, will overlook the law firm the founder used in favor of one strong in antitrust practice. The same for clients engaged in environmental disputes, public offerings, real estate syndications, and labor relations. Increasingly, the firms with the strongest presence in the various legal specialties get the call. A reputation as solid generalists—or for that matter as good squash players—is no longer enough to land and retain selective clients.

   But in creating practice boutiques, expansionary firms are obliged to raid competitors for partners and associates skilled in a smorgasbord of legal specialties. Attracting well-known practitioners brings the predator firm instant credibility, and in some cases instant clients, in the target markets.

   When New York's Shea & Gould, long regarded as a savvy, politically connected firm, decided in late 1984 to become a major player in Manhattan's booming real estate practice, it raided megafirm Weil, Gotshal & Manges, snaring its lead real estate gun, partner Charles Goldstein, and most of his 30-man department. Overnight, Shea & Gould became one of the city's premier real estate practitioners, adding substantially to its fee base and its potential for future earnings.

A successful coup, yes, but a kind of coup that is anathema to legal purists at the grand old firms. Talent raids (lawyers prefer the euphemism "lateral transfers") violate an archaic and somewhat emotional belief that a law firm should groom its associates and anoint its partners exclusively from within. While this is touted as a quality-control measure, its true appeal relates to the dated notion of the law firm as a club. If partnership is unrestricted, if outsiders are admitted for wanton commercial objectives, does membership retain its privileged status?

For Milbank, which had previously limited its lateral hires (called "parachutists" by the firm's reactionaries) to a few isolated cases, using them mostly to fill positions left vacant by death, illness, or retirement, Forger's plan to create practice boutiques threatened to disturb the almighty status quo.

■ Ditto for a Los Angeles merger. The move to multicity practice, spurred again by the more aggressive players among the giants, is based on the controversial notion that a firm skilled in lucrative practice specialties should extend beyond its home base, making its services available wherever its clients go— or really more than that, wherever sufficient work can be found for its lawyers whether it be from existing clients or those waiting to be tapped.

Until recently, firms serviced out-of-state clients by dispatching teams of lawyers to live out of suitcases until the matter was settled or by referring work to a network of friendly firms likely to return the favor on their home turf. But with corporate counsel now basing selections on expertise rather than cozy relationships, skilled newcomers can compete for business the very day they enter a market. Within months of christening its Los Angeles outpost, Skadden, Arps, the profession's premier merger and acquisition specialist, was busy claiming West Coast M&A business from established megafirm competitors.

Like the creation of in-house boutiques, branching is not entirely a home-grown effort. To establish immediate credibility in the adopted markets—and to gain local savvy that can be vital for dealing with judges and clients—the carpetbaggers prefer to put down their roots by merging with an established practice and only then gluing on a contingent of partners relocated from the home office.

"Approaching a new market lean and mean—that is by sending out a hearty contingent from the home office to establish a beachhead without bringing in outsiders—may appeal to those who want to preserve collegiality, but it doesn't work very well," Forger says. "Experience shows that to be successful in a sophisticated market, you need a critical mass of partners, associates, legal skills, and local knowledge. And you need it from the outset. Having a full mix of resources, a full contingent of lawyers, builds confidence and in turn attracts clients.

"Would six guys from Wall Street succeed in opening a Los Angeles office? Consider me skeptical. Far better, I believe, is to fuse with a group of local practitioners who can bring established clients to the table, or to merge with another firm. If there's a good fit between the lawyers, between the firms, you have strengths you couldn't possibly bring to the market singlehandedly."

True enough, but once again this doesn't sit well with those who exalt the virtues of law firm collegiality. If an isolated lateral transfer is sinful and is conducted only under extraordinary circumstances, gobbling up an entire firm, especially one with 80 to 100 lawyers, is blasphemy.

"This firm itself is the product of a merger between two New York practices,"* says a Milbank partner. "The only merger in our history, it occurred more than a half a century ago. But don't you know that some of the people here still talk about the problems in making the merger work, in making the pieces fit together? To hear them talk, you'd think it happened months ago."

■ Another business-minded innovation, paying annual bonuses to those ambitious associates churning out exceptionally high client billings, violates the ancient tradition of basing compensation solely on seniority. Under this "lockstep" ap-

---

*Masten & Nichols, where Hadley and Tweed were partners, and Murray, Aldrich & Webb, where Milbank was a partner. The merger occurred in 1931. The roots of the latter firm trace back to 1866, which Milbank partners now consider their firm's genesis.

proach, all of the lawyers entering a firm in a given year earn equal compensation throughout their careers. That a Type A partner is a talented workaholic who contributes substantially to the bottom line while his colleague, also a class of '62 Yalie, stopped superachieving the day he left law school is not reflected in their paychecks. Both are compensated equally.

True believers in the law firm as a club insist that this equality reinforces collegiality by discouraging lawyers within the same firm from competing with one another for higher pay or for the bragging rights that go with it. Those who've grown up with the system swear by it. This was evidenced by the shellacking a proposal to end lockstep, or at least to pepper it with incentives, suffered at the hands of the Milbank partnership in May 1984. The proposal, presented at the partners' annual meeting, called for a 16-point compensation formula keyed to a range of performance standards from rainmaking (attracting clients) to productivity. It was rejected overwhelmingly.

In hindsight, the issue was a dead duck before it came to a vote. A plurality of the partners were at or near the firm's lockstep maximum ($450,000), and these lawyers, mostly middle-aged and beyond, saw little reason to rewrite the rules in the winter of their careers. To do so would mean short-changing themselves to reward what most of the naysayers regarded as young Turks too impatient to wait their turn for the ultimate reward.

What's more, an incentive-based system keyed even minimally to rainmaking loomed as a threat to those partners who, supported as they were throughout their careers by Milbank's wealthy patron, Chase Manhattan Bank, had been spared the messy business of scrounging for clients. Why make that part of the rules now?

"In voting down incentive compensation, the partners said they would rather compete outside than inside the firm," Forger says, sounding from the frustration in his voice like a man who understands his colleagues and respects them for what they are, but wishes he could do more to change their way of thinking. "Collegiality is dear to them and they believe that lockstep fosters that quality."

Possibly, but it also discourages individual initiative. Highly motivated lawyers at Jones, Day, at Weil, Gotshal, and at the other megafirms that have rejected lockstep know that the more they put out for clients, the more they'll find in their pay envelopes. This kind of undiluted incentive boosts productivity and encourages more creative and responsive legal services. Precisely what today's independent corporate counsel are shopping for. And precisely what the living ghosts of law firms past want very much to prevent.

It falls to the managing partner to balance these opposing forces, and it is a delicate balance indeed. By rushing to erase the rules of the past, he invites a backlash that can undermine his ability to lead. On the other hand, by eschewing change in favor of tradition, he allows more aggressive practitioners to widen their lead over his firm and to court, with alarming success, what were once loyal patrons.

"We cannot pursue a policy of no growth," Forger admits, "because that leads inevitably to decline. Either you consciously press ahead or unwittingly fall behind. I won't preside over the latter."

Instead, he must use his position to nurture change—rather than ramrod it—through the Milbank hierarchy. Like his counterparts at other conservative firms struggling with sensitive and highly emotional issues, Forger knows he must function as a diplomat, paying homage to Milbank's traditions while simultaneously nudging the firm toward the hard realities of the late 20th century. An extraordinary challenge, but one that Forger appears capable of pulling off.

"Of all the major firms practicing today, only some are going to survive over the long term," he acknowledges. "By laying the foundation for geographic expansion and for the development of new practice departments, we are insuring our future. Our future success.

"How big will we grow? Some people here are betting we'll be 600 lawyers by 1990. Perhaps. Anything's possible. But while I can't make guarantees about our growth rate, there is one thing I'm dead certain of. Those firms that fail to keep up, that fail to adapt themselves to changes in the world around them, will be picked apart piece by piece by the bigger firms. Good people won't stay with losing ventures. Firms identified as losers will lose their clients, their partners, teams of partners. Before long they'll be shadows of their former selves.

"They won't, I'm afraid, be among the survivors."

3

In the Eye of the Storm: Shearman & Sterling and Citibank

"You spent a year of your life doing a stock syndication for a company that makes nondairy creamer!"

Susan Sarrandon to her
attorney husband (Edward Herrmann)
in the film *Compromising Positions*

Resistance to change hasn't spared the giant law firms.

"Last year, Arthur Field, our partner in charge of professional services, approached me with the idea of changing our in-house telephone directory to list all lawyers alphabetically without regard to rank," says Robert Carswell, senior partner of New York–based megafirm Shearman & Sterling. "That would put an end to the practice, one that went back for more years than I wished to count, of listing partners and associates separately.

"I thought Field's suggestion—which he said would 'bring us into the 20th century on this'—made good sense. Why make the partner-associate distinction in a phone directory? Everyone in the firm knows who the partners are, and clients, who also get the directory, don't really care. They call the lawyer they need for a particular matter, whatever his rank.

"So I suggested that Field air the idea with a few partners around the firm, see if anyone had any objections, and, if not, go ahead with it. Certainly, this wasn't going to bring monumental change to Shearman & Sterling. Or so I thought.

"When his informal poll failed to turn up serious objections, Field proceeded with the new directories, having them printed and distributed throughout the firm. And whambam, no sooner are they in circulation than I'm hearing all kinds of negative feedback.

"We found out, soon enough, that about 45 percent of the partners opposed the change. Some felt quite strongly about it, which they let me know point blank. If there's a lesson here, it's that change never comes easy to an institution built on traditions. But this conservatism isn't all bad. It has a way of protecting something very valuable."

Carswell, whose quiet, understated style makes for effective management in a complex firm, is struggling with much the same alligator that Alexander Forger is wrestling with. His firm, the only Wall Street banking practice among the giants, shares Milbank's cultural heritage and its association with a predominant client, Citibank, which has filled Shearman's coffers for 94 years.

Faced with sweeping changes in banking generally, at Citibank specifically (which accounts for about 25 percent of Shearman's $120 million in annual fees), and in the legal professions, the 112-year-old law firm is groping for answers, for ways to maintain growth without abandoning its strict interpretation of professional conduct and, along with that, its haughty elitism. While its position may be stronger than Milbank's—it has considerably more lawyers, a greater infrastructure, and a wider scope of practice—its future growth is in no way assured. A cloud of uncertainty hangs over the firm. How it fares will depend, to a great extent, on how effectively Carswell can de-institutionalize the institution, making it more of a hard-nosed business than a well-endowed men's club.

The cloud that looms over Shearman & Sterling is also its silver lining: Citicorp.* Spend an hour at either of Shearman's New York offices and you sense, as if shrouded in fog, the omnipresence of this dominating client. Both offices are ensconced in Citicorp buildings, at 53 Wall Street and One Citicorp Center, and both reflect the prevailing Citicorp statement in architecture and interior design. Downtown, Shearman's offices are a model of Wall Street drab—heavy

---

*Holding company for Citibank.

wood paneling, floor-to-ceiling drapes, traditional furniture. Uptown, in Citicorp's newer and glitzier digs, Shearman-the-chameleon opts for minimalism, reflecting the bankers' contemporary outlook. Clean lines, abstract art, lots of glass and mica.

But even here, the firm's ingrained conservatism shows through. "For some strange reason—which none of us, try as we might, can figure out—they wanted every darn floor in this place to look almost identical," says a grandmotherly-looking secretary in the midtown office. "Do you understand how confusing that can be? Get off the elevator at the wrong floor—a common mistake because the reception areas are alike—and you wind up returning to someone else's desk and working there until the legitimate owner returns to inform you that you're sitting in her seat. If you want to know the real meaning of 'embarrassment,' that's it. It makes you cringe."

Whether the partners find the right office or not—whether they're working in their own chairs or those of colleagues—chances are they're toiling away on Citibank matters. At one time or another most of the partners and a healthy (or unhealthy, depending on your point of view) contingent of associates find themselves immersed in some facet of the bank's legal affairs.

The firm is two-headed about this. On one side, it radiates pride over what is widely acknowledged as one of the most enduring and lucrative of all law firm–client relationships. As Citibank grew from the middle ranks of American banking to the number one spot, Shearman grew in tandem, exploding from 7 to 428 lawyers since the turn of the century. During the course of the relationship, which dates back to 1891 (then with Citibank's predecessor, National City Bank of New York), lawyer and client have viewed each other as family. A silver plate on permanent exhibition in Shearman's sixth-floor Wall Street reception area is signed by bank executives on the occasion of Shearman's 100th anniversary.

No doubt the relationship has been manna from heaven for Shearman & Sterling. No one is more aware of this than the partners. As they passed by the firm's Christmas tree after a long and particularly glowing holiday luncheon, the author overheard three partners—all north of 50—discussing Santa Claus.

PARTNER ONE: *(Points to a stack of boxes under the tree)*: Looks like Santa's brought some nice gifts this year.

PARTNER TWO: You know those boxes are empty.

PARTNER THREE: Right. The real gifts went over to the bank already.

PARTNER ONE: That's okay. We get our gifts from them the rest of
                 the year. (*All laugh.*)

Over the years, Shearman's Santa Claus has been more generous than
Saint Nick. Blessed with a virtual exclusive on Citibank's legal work,
Shearman has inherited a steady stream of banking transactions and
with it the opportunity to develop considerable expertise in a broad
spectrum of banking practices. Expertise that has brought hundreds of
coattail clients, mostly foreign banks (including Fuji Bank, Bank of
Nova Scotia, and Westdeutsche Landesbank), into the Shearman fold.
   But like all incestuous relationships, this one has not been spared
negative repercussions. By virtually guaranteeing a flow of uninter-
rupted work—and by assuring a minimum level of partnership
compensation—it has, according to some sources, fostered bad habits.
In some quarters, Shearman's image is that of a firm that throws hordes
of partners and associates at work that could be performed by half as
many professionals, of a living, breathing anachronism whose billing
is out of whack with modern cost-benefit analyses, and of a firm that
is better at spending its inheritance than creating a fortune of its own.
With little competition externally (as one Shearman partner puts it,
"We *are* Citibank's lawyers") and internally (lockstep sees to that),
the partners have grown fat around the middle.
   "Those Shearman & Sterling guys were far removed from the real
world, meaning everything beyond Citicorp's doors," says a former
Shearman associate who is now a partner with New York's Parker
Chapin Flattau & Klimpl. "I was involved in some work the firm did
for a middle-sized family-owned business based in Manhattan. I don't
recall how they came to hire Shearman, but boy, were they miserable
that they did once the bills came in. I learned from the president's son
that the old man nearly had a coronary when he saw the invoices. It
seemed that Shearman had commissioned a battalion of associates for
what these guys were accustomed to having one, maybe two lawyers
handle. What really pissed them off was that the legal bills far exceeded
their exposure in the case.
   "Needless to say, they'd never go back to the firm, but I don't
think Shearman recognizes that even to this day. They're too accus-

tomed to dealing with a captive client. They think everyone comes back—that it's just a matter of time.''

While the loss of a minuscule client is hardly a threat to the mighty Shearman & Sterling, the attitude that caused the rift may yet haunt it. Gearing a practice to a dominant client and assuming that client is in fact captive is risky pool in an increasingly competitive and thoroughly irreverent market.

''When X client supplies a firm with millions or perhaps tens of millions of dollars in fees, it is entirely possible for that firm to get complacent,'' says Henry King, managing partner of Wall Street's stalwart Davis Polk & Wardwell, lead counsel for the investment banking house of Morgan Stanley & Co.* Like Alexander Forger, his neighbor in New York's One Chase Manhattan Plaza, King (elected to his post in May 1984) is acting as a catalyst for change. ''Complacency is a word I don't want included in this firm's vocabulary. That's because it's a trap. Anyone who ever thought they could rest on their laurels, who ever believed they could take a client's business for granted, has learned by now—or soon will—what a mistake that is.''

The trap is in thinking that the client will forever view the law firm as part of the family, treating it with the deference afforded a close relative. When this tightly knit relationship begins to unravel, when the client begins to apply to the acquisition of legal services the same business discipline it brings to the purchase of paper clips, complacency takes its toll. The once-coddled firm is stricken by the change, partly because it never believed change would occur and even more because it feels incapable of replacing the business it will lose as the client calls on a wider range of firms.

Thus Shearman's growing ambivalance with Mother Bank. Although Citibank continues to dole out most of its work to S & S, rumors that this fossilized relationship is slated for wholesale change are giving Shearman partners cause for concern.

Concern set in when Citicorp chairman and Shearman loyalist Walter Wriston retired from the bank in August 1984, anointing as his replacement John Reed, a vice chairman 20 years his junior who was feared throughout the bank as a relentless cost cutter. Pragmatic, tough-minded, unwilling to accept the bank-as-a-bureaucracy syndrome that is

---

*His comments referred to law firms in general, not to Shearman & Sterling specifically.

tolerated in similar financial institutions, Reed had earned his stripes by bringing a strict, bottom-line orientation to Citicorp's consumer division. His election being viewed as a clear mandate to spread this management style to every corner of the bank—including the commercial divisions where Shearman historically earned the great bulk of its fees —the rise of Mr. Reed was greeted with considerable angst at 53 Wall. With S & S claiming about half* of Citicorp's $42 million in outside legal bills—and with Reed, unlike many of the bank's senior executives, having no ties to the law firm—the cause for concern was apparent.

"Every corporation of any size has pockets of waste, little islands of employees whose only function is to collect their paychecks and add unnecessarily to the bottom line," says a Citicorp vice president. "And we're no exception. We must have a thousand people or more who while away their mornings in the bathroom reading the *Daily News*, who take two-hour lunches pouring over the *Post* and then spend the afternoon getting ready to go home. But I must say we've had much less of that since Reed became an officer of the bank. He's a cost cutter extraordinaire. Every function, every job, every service under his charge has to be justified for cost and efficiency. If not, out comes the hatchet and away goes the fat.

"Reed's mission—his brilliance, I might add—is to find more efficient ways of accomplishing the bank's business. Now, I don't pretend to know all that much about lawyers or what they charge, but I've rubbed elbows with maybe a half-dozen Shearman & Sterling partners over the course of my career, and I keep hearing these little jibes directed at them about the rich getting richer. It's easy to understand. You sit across the table from them at one of those banker-borrower-lawyer marathons and you can tell, just by the quality of their suits or maybe a certain smugness, that they're outearning you four or five times over. I can't say I ever felt bitterness about it, but some pangs of jealousy? Hell, I'm only human.

"Maybe that's why I felt this inner satisfaction when word leaked out that their meal ticket was about to expire. The scuttlebutt started shortly after Reed became chairman. No official announcement, mind you. Just the old, uncannily reliable rumor mill predicting the fall of the Shearman dynasty."

---

*The firm also collects substantial fees from borrowers involved in Citicorp transactions, who are required to pay the law firm directly.

Accurate or not, this is precisely the kind of talk that makes Shearman's high command break out in cold sweats. The fear, which some will admit behind closed doors, is that prophecies have a way of fulfilling themselves—that Citibank's managers, embarrassed by their apparent reliance on Shearman, will be provoked into making faster and more sweeping changes than even a budgetarian of Reed's caliber would have contemplated. With the press focusing on the Citicorp-Shearman relationship—and with bankers looking in print like lambs being taken routinely to slaughter—the lawyers fear that change is inevitable.

This fear intensified when the October '84 issue of the *American Lawyer* carried a front-page bombshell—"Is Shearman & Sterling's Golden Goose Getting Restless"—telling the world that Reed-managed Citibank was quietly reevaluating its legal affairs with an eye toward shifting more of its business away from Shearman & Sterling.

Shearman's partners seethed over this passage:

> Are good skills and quality work enough to keep a solid grasp on such an aggressive client? Over the past decade, Citicorp—in large part through its myriad Citibank subsidiaries—has expanded the frontiers of commercial and consumer banking. Yet, from interviews with Citicorp executives, in-house counsel and former Shearman & Sterling and Citicorp lawyers, it appears that Shearman & Sterling is not keeping up. As executives have pushed harder to widen the scope of commercial banking, Citicorp insiders charge, Shearman & Sterling has answered their probing questions with conservative and indecisive opinions. As the bank and their own clients have become increasingly cost conscious, they say, Shearman & Sterling has resisted pressure to cut costs. And, perhaps most significantly, in the bank's consumer-oriented division, which has begun to surpass the institutional division in growth and importance, Shearman & Sterling has not held onto its usual share of the work.
>
> *American Lawyer*,
> October 1984, p. 133,
> by Ellen Joan
> Pollock.

Questioned about the piece soon after its publication, Shearman partners reeled off a stream of obscenities aimed not as much at the reporting as at the impact it would have on the bank.

"Look, Reed's only human," said a Shearman partner who agreed to talk "providing my name never gets beyond these walls." "He's bound to get a copy of that scandal sheet—no doubt half of our competitors have already slipped one into his mailbox—and when he does he'll see a very flattering portrait of a cost-conscious CEO pitted against a gluttonous leech determined to siphon away his corporate profits with staggering legal bills. That's goddam rubbish, and I think he knows it. Were we even remotely as inflexible as that article inferred, we'd have been Citibank's 'former' lawyers for years now.

"But what concerns us is that the article creates a damaging image—not only for Shearman & Sterling but equally for Reed and the bank. It makes it sound as if they're completely remiss in continuing to work with us. More than remiss—a goddam laughing stock. I don't mean to imply that Reed doesn't have a mind of his own, but let's not hide behind the manure pile. We all know these articles can build a head of steam. They have a way of forcing events. How's Reed supposed to respond when another CEO asks if he's still using that 'dull, conservative law firm'?"

The partner's gripe underlines a glaring weakness at S & S—one that has more to do with image making than law or banking. After practicing for a century in relative obscurity, the venerable law firms, Shearman included, have recently been subject to penetrating coverage from the business press and from a cadre of mild to muckraking legal publications. Squarely in the muckraking column, the *American Lawyer*, launched in 1978 by author Steven Brill, has stunned the profession by digging deep into the firms' once-private affairs and coming up with more dirty laundry than the *National Enquirer* has on Princess Di. In the process, it has become the journalistic scapegoat lawyers love to hate: every giant law firm partner questioned about it claimed to detest "the scandal sheet," while to a man each had the latest issue atop his desk.

The power of the publication is that it is widely read (by clients and lawyers alike) and widely quoted. In the weeks immediately following the "Golden Goose" piece, partners at four of the giant firms (Weil, Gotshal; Skadden, Arps; Jones, Day; and Finley, Kumble) volunteered their impression—as if Brill the puppeteer was moving their lips—that Citicorp was breaking away from Shearman & Sterling.

In the midst of a wide-ranging interview in his corner office atop 919 Third Avenue, a senior Skadden, Arps partner points a finger at the Citicorp Center, a prominent Manhattan tower that rises from the skyline to the right of his sprawling desk. "No one has a lock and key on clients anymore. I can tell you that Citibank will gradually be moving more and more of its legal work away from Shearman & Sterling to other firms, ours included. Someday soon when you say Citibank you won't automatically think Shearman & Sterling. They're a fine law firm, and I don't want to disparage them, but things are coming unglued over there. That relationship—as we've all come to know it—is history."

Whether this hopeless picture is entirely accurate is a matter of opinion. The *American Lawyer*, its high standards notwithstanding, is given to occasional excesses. But regardless of who turns out to be right—the Shearman partners or the journalists—the episode reveals Shearman's weakness in dealing with the object of its greatest animosity, the press.

Here again, the legacy of a shielded and privileged past works against the law firm. Although the new breed of legal reporters have been snooping around in earnest for five years now and although their publications have gained substantial clout with corporate decision makers (those who acquire legal services), Shearman has failed to develop an intelligent policy for dealing with them. While some of the most successful attorneys of the decade—Skadden, Arps's Joe Flom and Weil, Gotshal's Ira Millstein among them—owe a good measure of their prominence to savvy media relations, Shearman has stuck its head in the sand hoping it will all go away.

Weeks after the *American Lawyer* broke the "Golden Goose" story, Robert Knight, then Shearman's senior partner, held an interview with the author of this book. Incensed at the allegations of a rift between S & S and Citicorp he was tense, short-tempered, sharp-tongued. Clearly, he detested the assignment but pressed ahead, goaded into service by partner David McCabe, the firm's media flack catcher. If there were inaccuracies in the *American Lawyer* story, the interview afforded him the opportunity to set the record straight. But the managing partner had something else in mind.

Seated in the inner room of an elegant office suite—McCabe at his side—Knight greets his visitor with a terse broadside that all questions concerning Citicorp are off limits.

With one brush, Knight excludes from the agenda Shearman's premier client, one that to many is the firm's body and soul. That this is a public relations fiasco is painfully clear to lieutenant McCabe, who arranged the interview and who now squirms in his seat as if his dentist was drilling into a root canal.

In place of Citibank, Knight suggests that the interview focus on the firm's pro bono work. Hardly germane to the central policies and personality of a dynastic law firm whose history is inexorably tied to the lucrative and highly uncharitable world of money center banking. And although Knight ultimately commented on lockstep, lateral hiring, and the state of the legal profession, his remarks were terse.

Dressed in an English-cut navy blue pin striped suit, Shearman's senior partner, deep into the third and last year of his reign, resembled a Dickensian curmudgeon berating a trembling clerk who'd come before him for a raise. Ensconced behind his desk (shrouded in the haze of a half-dozen filter cigarettes), he appeared to be a living symbol of the Shearman culture—a culture that prompts a 64-year-old man indoctrinated in the wisdom of lockstep and accustomed to thinking of the law firm as the continuation of academia to refer to colleagues not as partners but as classmates.

Within weeks of the interview, Knight completed his tenure as senior partner and stepped down from the management post.* Days later, a sheepish Dave McCabe calls the author.

McCABE: Hey, you really picked a bad time to come up here. Everyone was a little touchy what with that *American Lawyer* thing and all.

STEVENS: I noticed.

McCABE: Look, let's get you back in here. You know Bob Carswell's our new senior partner. I think you'll find him a good deal more—how shall I say—accessible. Don't let the last experience color your opinion of us.

Enter Robert Carswell, a Brooklyn-born Harvard man, sometime lawyer sometime bureaucrat, whose professional career has alternated between the Shearman & Sterling partnership and government service, including a four-year stint as Deputy Treasury Secretary in the Carter Administration. Having held down that hot seat through the politically

---

* He remains with the firm as a partner.

sensitive Chrysler bailout and the Iranian hostage crisis (including the freezing of Iran's U.S. assets), Carswell emerged as the ideal candidate to guide S & S through a decade of change that will alter the firm's culture and, in turn, test its mettle as a partnership.

Trained in the great cauldron of politics, he brings real-world experience to the job of managing a law firm that some say is as much an institution as the Treasury Department. Clearly, the Washington years have made the man a politician in his own right. Asked how he will guide Shearman & Sterling on the fundamental issues of lockstep, mergers, laterals, and marketing, he treads softly, ever mindful of the collective psyche.

"I don't think the divine answer to any of these questions has yet come down from the heavens. There's no right way and no wrong way. It's a matter of what the partnership thinks best. I know they'll act at the appropriate time."

Perhaps, but Carswell also knows that waiting for divine answers to "come down from the heavens" is not leadership. And that change—consciously managed change—is essential to a law firm's vitality. While he gives lip service to preserving the culture ("conservatism . . . has a way of protecting something very valuable"), he subtly alerts the partnership to the danger of inaction (as Henry King calls it, "the trap of complacency").

"In Washington, emergencies are the mother of invention," Carswell says. "Problems that go unnoticed for years get attention only when there's a crisis. Hardly the ideal time to effect intelligent change. By then, the thing's blown up in your face."

Carswell's style, honed during his Treasury years, appears to be one of quietly seeking change without announcing that change is in the offing. Questioned about his management plans, he responds diplomatically, paying homage to Shearman's ancient culture while revealing his willingness to depart from it. Reading between the lines, one gets the distinct impression that under Carswell, Shearman & Sterling will act to insure its place among the survivors.

Carswell on lockstep:

"I see no reason to discard the lockstep system. We don't want our youngsters competing against each other in the early years.

"But let me add that lockstep isn't sacrosanct. We depart from it now and then to recognize truly exceptional performance. By the same token, when older partners get less productive, we adjust their compensation accordingly. Not that we take the axe to them—that's not our style—but their earnings are reduced.

"Let's face it, every firm, each at its own pace, will have to move away from lockstep eventually. It can't last forever. Today's competitive market, with its emphasis on efficiency, just won't allow it."

Carswell on multicity practice:

"There's a new truism in the legal profession that clients want the same law firms to represent them wherever they do business. To hold on to these clients, the thinking goes, law firms must establish multicity practices, matching their clients city for city, branch for branch.

"Well, maybe that's true, and maybe I'll wind up with egg on my face for doubting it, but I don't buy it. I'm not at all certain that clients want the same law firms shadowing them across the globe, and I'm equally uncertain as to whether we should automatically pick up and go where they do.

"This is not to say that there isn't legitimate reason to open offices in major commercial centers. Providing it meets certain business and professional criteria, geographic expansion may be right for law firms. The question is, how much expansion? In what kind of framework? With what limitations?

"Twenty cities? Thirty? I don't think that's for us. Unbridled growth comes at the expense of quality—a sacrifice we're not willing to make. But limited expansion, that's a different matter. We've opened domestic offices in San Francisco and Los Angeles, and I can't say we'll necessarily stop there. We're not afraid to act when there's legitimate reason to do so."

The LA move shows how decisively Shearman & Sterling can break through a culture barrier when patron saint Citicorp beckons. A move infinitely more complex than changing telephone listings was marked by little of the petty carping that poisoned that silly affair. As much as the Shearman culture resists change, it makes an exception when its bread and butter is at stake.

In 1984, Citicorp began relocating its western energy lending operation from New York, where Shearman had handled the work since its inception, to Los Angeles. Because it preferred to have local counsel on hand for this work, Citicorp invited Shearman to open an LA office of its own or—horror of horrors—risk losing the business to an indigenous firm.

"Although the discussions were kept secret," says a partner with a megafirm competitor, "anyone even remotely familiar with either Shearman & Sterling or the bank would have been surprised—make that 'shocked'—if they hadn't talked about relocating altogether. Considering that they go back to about 800 B.C., it came under the heading of standard operating procedure.

"The prospective relocation riled some of Shearman's conservatives-in-residence who resented the idea of acting with a gun to their heads, the gun being the threat of losing Citicorp business, and others who weren't certain a Los Angeles office was right for the firm. But wiser heads—in this case the vast majority of partners—prevailed and fired back a verbal telegram that yes, Los Angeles would be a delightful place to practice. This, let no one forget, was Citibank calling, and Shearman isn't in the habit of saying no to them.

"And something else was at work here. The way I see it, Shearman & Sterling's leadership exhibited, perhaps for the first time, real sensitivity to Citibank's capacity for independence. They recognized that Los Angeles is dangerous territory, a real competitive quagmire. Home base for some substantial law firms, namely Gibson, Dunn and O'-Melveny & Myers, it is also home to multicity practitioners—yes, the same Gibson & O'Melveny. With these West Coast infiltrators now practicing out of New York branch offices, they are in post position to serve Los Angeles clients on both coasts, something Shearman could not do until it opened up out there.

"Today, mission one for major law firms is to protect their bases. Even Shearman recognizes that. Should a bicoastal firm get cozy with Citibank in Los Angeles by accepting business Shearman refuses to take, it has a natural entrée to at least part of the bankers' business in New York. Open the door a crack and there's no telling how wide it will swing.

"Don't let them tell you differently. This was on Shearman's mind when they decided to set up shop in Los Angeles."

Carswell, whose occasional bursts of candor are apparently unrivaled in Shearman's long history, admits as much in revealing the firm's broad-based motives for going west.

"We agreed to open in Los Angeles for three reasons," Carswell says, running his hand over his head, patting down occasional tumbleweeds of dry, flyaway hair. "Most important, although none of the local firms could match our expertise in oil and gas financing, they had incentive aplenty to come up to speed and compete with us for that business. We saw that as cause to protect our flank. And there were other factors

- "With Wall Street's investment banking houses branching out to California, we recognized a need to serve them on both coasts.
- "We identified Los Angeles as a potential staging area for Pacific Basin business."

Clearly an offensive and defensive strategy. By planting its flag in Los Angeles, Shearman built a chain link fence around the bank's West Coast business, keeping its hooks in one of Citicorp's fastest-growing markets. By going along with Citicorp, the firm could open its LA branch—which it was under increasing competitive pressure to do—with the guarantee of substantial fees from day one. A low-risk strategy that is central to the Shearman culture.

Of all Shearman's many services to the bank, none is more critical than debt restructuring. And more than any other, the debt practice illustrates how the megafirms become intermingled in their clients' most sensitive affairs and how this perpetuates the myth of indispensability.

For Shearman & Citibank, debt restructuring achieved critical proportions with Mexico's shocking announcement in August 1982 that it could not make payments on billions of dollars in foreign debt held by about 800 banks, mostly in the U.S. and Europe. Brought to its knees by a worldwide oil glut, falling energy prices, capital flight, inflation, and rising interest rates, Mexico was on the brink of financial disaster.

News of the crisis sent shock waves to Manhattan, first to Citicorp—which had more than $3 billion in questionable loans extended to Mexico (more than any other bank)—and then, in a frantic SOS, to Shearman & Sterling.

"No matter how the official announcement was worded, the message from the Mexicans was cold and blunt: 'We're broke,' " Carswell recalls. "For the banks at risk this could be disastrous—even life-threatening."

On the day of the announcement, Mexico's major creditors—a Who's Who of money center banks including Citicorp, Chemical, Chase Manhattan, and the Bank of America—formed a 13-member advisory group charged with representing all of the creditor banks in negotiations with the Mexican government. The three co-chairs were Citibank, Bank of America, and the Swiss Bank Corporation. Influenced no doubt by Citibank, they retained Shearman & Sterling as the group's counsel.

Events moved quickly from there. On Labor Day weekend Carswell, accompanied by Shearman's lead partner for Mexican debt rescheduling Alfred Mudge, flew to Toronto, where the pair joined Citicorp's chief rescheduling officer William Rhodes and chairman Wriston at the annual meeting of the World Bank and the International Monetary Fund. Here the 13 advisory group members began drafting emergency measures to deal with Mexico's huge and potentially devastating default. Behind closed doors, plans were laid to assure the banking community's very survival. Shearman partners, who contributed ideas of their own, were the only nonbankers privy to the discussions.

Through its Citibank connection, the firm found itself hot-wired into an explosive sector of banking practice. Quickly the debt problem, and the opportunities it created, mushroomed. In the months following the Mexican crisis, the cancer of fiscal insolvency spread through Latin America, with 14 nations including Brazil, Bolivia, Argentina, and Venezuela defaulting or threatening default on their loans. Stunned by the specter of a massive default, the international banking community circled the wagons, working collectively to prevent a wholesale disaster that could cripple the world economy. Just keeping the system intact would require round-the-clock efforts both by the bankers and the lawyers pressed close to their sides.

For Shearman, which played grim-faced to Citibank's near panic, the crises spelled W-I-N-D-F-A-L-L. With the bankers' bare butts exposed to the equatorial sun like a gringo's wallet on a Tijuana sidestreet, the call went out for lawyers, teams of lawyers, holy swarms of attorneys, barristers, counselors—most of whom carried the imprimatur of Shearman & Sterling. Within two years of the first Mexican tremor, the firm added nine bank advisory groups to its client list (eight in Latin America, one in Africa), representing in each case both the group collectively and Citicorp as a prominent member. Clearly, Shearman was harvesting the fruits of megafirm status and of a possibly endangered but still wildly profitable relationship.

By all accounts, Shearman's work on the reschedulings was first rate: precise, accurate, technically sound. But did it contribute materially to the clients' success or lack of it? Did it provide a legitimate test of a law firm's competence? Its indispensability?

The great paradox of debt restructuring, as it pertains to sovereign nations, is that law firms must forgo what is traditionally their most potent weapon, the threat of court action. This became painfully obvious from the earliest days of the Mexican crisis. Fearing that drastic action would push the debtor into an irreversible slide—or worse yet that the government would simply throw up its hands and refuse to pay—the bankers embarked on a policy of appeasement, extending Mexico's credit rather than accelerating the payment of its outstanding loans. While creditors in domestic cases can seek relief under the bankruptcy laws, those involved in international transactions are often limited to negotiated settlements. Here, the litigator's job is stay out of court.

But the black hole of the Mexican crisis kept getting bigger and bigger. In November of '82 a letter of intent was announced between Mexico and the International Monetary Fund, granting the debtor access to an extended funds facility* for 1983 to 1985. But this was predicated on the banking community's willingness to extend to Mexico another $5 billion in new loans.

"This demand was unprecedented, but the banks had little choice but to agree to it," says Mudge, arguably the world's most astute practitioner in debt reschedulings, who'd previously cut his teeth on similar reschedulings in Turkey and Zaire. "We worked from the end of 1982 to March of '83 putting together the new money agreement for the additional $5 billion. It was a massive undertaking, involving 526 banks and nine different currencies."

With this exhaustive and highly lucrative assignment complete, Shearman then worked with the Mexican advisory group in drawing

---

* A commitment by the IMF to extend financing to a country provided the country complies with certain performance criteria.

up model restructure agreements for Mexico's 52 public sector borrowers that had debt falling due between August '82 and December '84. The three biggest debtors—the United Mexico States (Mexican government), Pemex, the national oil company, and Nafinfa, a bank —were tackled first and signed on August 26, 1983. Work on the remaining 49 extended to the end of 1984.

In the meantime, the hungry mouth opened wider. "During this period it became clear that Mexico would need additional funds for 1984," Mudge says. "Again the banks came up with the money, committing an additional $3.8 billion."

In this thing up to their eyeballs already, the banks had no alternative but to continue shoveling money into the abyss. With $48 billion in debt falling due in the period from 1985 to 1990, it was clear that Mexico could not honor its obligations without further concessions. In July and August of 1984, the advisory group, acting as always for the banking community, negotiated a "financing principles proposal" that, to all intents and purposes, further appeased the debtor. The three-part proposal called for:

- Token prepayment of $1.2 billion of the first $5 billion in additional funding
- Extension of the 52 restructure agreements, postponing their maturities from 1987 through 1990 to 1998–99
- Extension of the maturities originally falling due in 1985 to 1990

Clearly, the bankers were dealing with default by extending additional credit. Adding fuel to the fire?

"That's one way of looking at it," says a partner with another Wall Street law firm also active in debt reschedulings. Like most of his colleagues, he demanded anonymity when talking about Citicorp. "But if you don't help the borrower get back on his feet—if you don't keep those talks alive—you run the risk of walking away from the table with your pockets turned inside out. Additional loans, extended to keep the debtors in business and to demonstrate good will from its fat-cat American bankers, is viewed as an investment that, if all goes well, will yield the bulk of the outstanding funds. It's a way of extending yourself not for the sake of the debtor, but ultimately to protect your own interests. And Shearman did a good job in protecting Citi-corp's interests. It knew the issues cold and built maximum protections into the new loan agreements.''

Shearman's job was to build into the loan extensions the following covenants designed to afford the bankers that vital protection:

- Negative pledges forbidding the borrowers to encumber their assets, save for those exceptions listed in the agreements
- Reporting provisions requiring the Mexican borrowers to make periodic reports on their economic and financial situation
- Events of default, which in theory give the banks the right to accelerate their debt if the borrower fails to pay interest or principal

Note the key words ''in theory.'' All the legalese Shearman could hurl at the problem wasn't going to change the fact that the bankers were in this thing to achieve a settlement at virtually any price save total loss of their loan portfolio. Faced with imminent default, they chose to extend rather than accelerate Mexico's debt. This policy would not be changed, legal agreements notwithstanding.

''You have to understand that these bankers were having night-mares over the foreign debt problem,'' says the Wall Street partner. ''For the first time in their careers, they could actually envision their bank going under—and with it their careers.

''This hit home to me one night after a banker's convention. After an exhaustive marathon of meetings, I had dinner with a banker friend staying at the same hotel, a guy involved in the foreign debt problems.

''We parted company at 9:30, vowing to catch up on some sorely needed sleep. Around 1 A.M., the air conditioning in my room goes on the blink, leaving the place like a high-rise sauna. After about a half-dozen fruitless calls to the front desk, I head downstairs to find someone, anyone, who can turn the unit back on, change my room, whatever. . . .

''Anyway, I'm walking through the lobby, and surprise, there's the banker, curled up in a club chair trying to sleep, a folded *Wall Street Journal* under his head. At first he makes a lame excuse about coming down for a pack of cigarettes, but seeing that won't fly, and apparently pleased to get this thing off his chest, he admits to such a bad case of the nerves that he can't sleep. The guy fears not only for the fate of his own bank but for the world banking system. He says he's watched the dawn come up every day since the crisis broke. Until then, I don't think I'd really gauged the depth of his concern.''

In this bizarre legal environment, where clients are literally fearful of alienating their adversaries, what is the lawyers' role? To a great extent it is that of a corporate security blanket—a role Shearman & Sterling has had nearly a century to perfect. In this capacity Shearman—and those other firms blessed, or cursed, with similar relationships—creates the illusion of indispensability. Not only from the quality of its work but from the comfort clients take in having trusted counsel at their side in times of crisis. This psychological factor perpetuates more of the traditional lawyer-client relationships than either side cares to admit. Citicorp executives accustomed to having a Shearman partner at the table simply prefer to face adversity with that kind of familiar support. That an avowed cost cutter like John Reed will continue to pay the price for this crutch is uncertain, but for the time being Shearman will continue to perpetuate the image of unswerving loyalty.

"When Citicorp asked us to advise them on the debt reschedulings, there was no question as to whether or not we should set up a practice unit to handle the matter," Carswell says, "only how quickly we could do it. Our client's interests were at stake. That's all we needed to know."

Amen.

To their credit, Shearman's top managers responded to Citicorp's concerns in the only way that would assure the bankers of quality legal counsel. An elite corps of partners and associates experienced in banking practice, some with previous experience in sovereign debt rescheduling, was shaped into a well-coordinated and highly specialized SWAT team that met with military precision Monday mornings in Conference Room 30A in Shearman's Citicorp Center offices.

Joined by Citicorp executives, some of whom needed only to board an elevator to attend, the team held roundtable discussions, reviewing the status of loan negotiations nation by nation while simultaneously exploring underlying economic conditions, tax implications, and regulatory issues.

"We wanted to bring uniformity to what had become a firmwide effort,'' Carswell says. "By bringing our people together in one room—people who at other times were spread across the map—and by going around the table with each one telling the others what he was up to and what he'd observed, we hoped to avoid getting tangled up in our own knots.

"The more we talked things over, the more we recognized that some common threads ran through the reschedulings. In the regulatory area, for example, questions about lending limits and reserve requirements had to be answered in every country. With this in mind, we were concerned not to reinvent the wheel . . . not to have a lawyer come up with something good in one country that we preceded not to use in another. Or to have one partner seek a regulatory ruling in one nation that would adversely affect our strategy in another. Sharing information, we knew, would be the best defense against this kind of damaging overlap. We wanted the team to perform to the highest possible standards. They had to. There was an awful lot at stake.''

Shearman's resolve in quickly dedicating a team of lawyers to an emerging practice opportunity was at once atypical and thoroughly in character. While the firm ordinarily shies away from marketing adventures, it is quick to respond to invitations from its chief benefactor.

But without a guaranteed return on its investment, it is unlikely that Shearman would have created a debt rescheduling practice of this magnitude. Not if it had to compete for the business without a built-in advantage. And therein lies the rub. While guarantees can bring financial rewards, they can also reinforce bad habits. Accustomed to a sure and immediate payback, the pampered firm often finds itself unwilling or unable to engage in dicier pursuits—a course it may be forced to follow when the "Golden Goose" no longer lays its precious eggs. Or when the client recognizes that the law firm is not, in fact, indispensable.

"Shearman and Sterling got that foreign debt work by being in the right place at the right time,'' says a Skadden, Arps partner. "Good for them. But they'd better recognize that it's going to be harder and harder to earn a living that way in this profession. In this business.''

4

Breaking "The Code": Finley, Kumble and the Cult of the Rainmakers

"As we enter a time when law firms are forced to become more competitive and marketing oriented, the winners will demonstrate two characteristics: they'll have prepared themselves for a competitive environment and they'll perform their marketing with style."

Bruce D. Heintz, national
director, Arthur Young Law Firms Group

Steve Kumble, 52, graduate of Yale University and Harvard Law School, managing partner of Finley, Kumble, Wagner, Heine, Underberg, Manley & Casey and architect of a new breed of national law firm, sits on a sofa in his Park Avenue office puffing smugly on a long tapered cigar. Stylishly preened from his manicured fingernails to meticulously coiffed salt-and-pepper mane, he looks and talks more like a Madison Avenue account executive than a prominent attorney. Perhaps because he thinks more like one.

While controversy surrounding his firm swirls through the legal profession—while competitors, clients, academics, and assorted observers of the megafirms question aloud whether Finley, Kumble can survive (praying in some quarters that it does not)—Steve Kumble ignores it all, assured that "the essential truth" will prevail:

"Clients have always left their law firms for one reason or another and will continue to do so," Kumble explains, resplendent in his powder blue shirt with yellow pin-dot tie and matching handkerchief. "That will never change. They'll leave because they're dissatisfied with fees, with the level of service, or with a lack of key legal skills that are critical to their businesses.

"We don't care which of these factors—be it one or a combination—causes the split. Whatever, we'll be there waiting to serve that client and to serve him better than ever before. We have the organization, the geographic coverage, and the practice capabilities to do just that. We've been working for almost 20 years to be in this position."

Kumble's cocky self-confidence is drawn from the conviction that time is on his side—that lawyer-client relationships based more on blind loyalty than on performance will continue to unravel and that those firms best positioned to provide skilled and efficient services will pick up the slack. To this way of thinking, the qualities that once made for successful law firms have become, in an increasingly competitive and demanding marketplace, disabling weaknesses. While Shearman & Sterling's Bob Carswell holds that resistance to change "has a way of protecting something very valuable," Kumble sees it as mental atrophy. And while Milbank, Tweed boasts of its service to three generations of Rockefellers (and as many generations of Chase Bank executives), Kumble volunteers that his firm hasn't been in business long enough to be imprisoned by tradition.

"Precisely because we have no history to speak of, and no rules that date back to the dark ages, we've been able to do whatever we've thought appropriate—and we've been able to do it quickly and in a rather unfettered way. There've been no protests from the ghosts of the past."

Derided by his peers as a P. T. Barnum of the legal profession—more of a showman than a skilled legal practitioner—Kumble is, in fact, a master marketer whose extraordinary success in building Finley, Kumble from eight founding lawyers in 1968 to more than 520 in 1985 is attributable to a simple but ingenious plan: to consciously violate the "gentlemanly" traditions held sacred by the incumbent practitioners in the top echelons of corporate law. With virtually all of the prominent and well-connected firms clinging to self-imposed restraints in the use of business-minded management procedures—and in responding to the nascent independence of corporate counsel—Kumble recognized that by breaking with tradition, by being among the first to trade marketing for mystique, he could position Finley, Kumble at the cutting edge of the legal revolution, giving it instant appeal to those clients who viewed "tradition" as a euphemism for "sleepy, stodgy, and expensive."

Like all true innovators, Kumble began by asking "Why not?" Why not recruit lateral associates and partners skilled in practice disciplines sought after in the marketplace? Why not establish branches beyond the firm's founding office in a Manhattan townhouse at 17 East 63rd Street? Why not create a truly national practice with offices in all of the major business centers? Why not merge with other firms if that promised exceptional growth? Why not pay lawyers for their initiative and performance even if that meant some earned substantially more than others?

The only answers Kumble found were vague and ambiguous rationalizations that talked not to the clients' needs but instead to the law firms' goal of perpetuating genteel practices. Taking this as a green light to proceed with his master plan, Kumble set out to replace the traditional law firm with one driven by business principles. Imitating Procter & Gamble in its heyday as a packaged goods marketer, Finley, Kumble scanned the market for business opportunities, seizing on them with a creativity and aggressiveness uncharacteristic of law firms. If others in the profession were content to wait for clients to knock on the door, content to sleep on the job, to rest on past glories, Kumble would profit from their complacency, outpacing competitors with a century's lead on the brash upstart.

Many can argue with Kumble's tactics, but few can argue with his success. In the 18 years since its founding, Finley, Kumble has soared to the ranks of the legal giants, practicing through a network of offices in New York, Los Angeles, Beverly Hills, San Diego, Newport Beach, Washington, D.C., Miami, and Baltimore. The firm boasts the full complement of megafirm services including general corporate law, securities, real estate, litigation, taxes, banking, labor, bankruptcy, energy, and, as icing on the cake, a strong LA-based entertainment practice. Wherever there are clients, wherever there is growth, promise, or opportunity in the legal marketplace, there is also Finley, Kumble.

The firm has achieved its explosive growth by creating and then staying loyal to the following growth tactics:

■ Much as Procter & Gamble built its dynasty by identifying breaking trends in the household products market, Finley, Kumble keeps its ear to the ground for those legal services (e.g., real estate and municipal finance) that are poised to catch fire with corporate clients. With the target in its sights, Finley draws a straight line to the marketplace, quickly hiring laterals blessed with the right expertise and, more often than not, with a built-in client following to assure immediate fees. Instantly, Finley, Kumble becomes a factor in the market.

"The new wrinkle in the law business today is that teams of lawyers at various firms are ready and willing to switch their affiliation for a higher bid," says Alexander Forger. "It wasn't long ago that headhunters played a minor role in this profession. Now they call almost daily with news that 12 real estate lawyers in Los Angeles or nine tax attorneys in New York are looking to leave their current firms to find fame and fortune elsewhere. This gives expansion-minded firms a unique opportunity to gain an instant presence in some very lucrative practices."

■ Just as corporations have shifted increasingly to large, national accounting firms, Kumble has acted on the premise, still a controversial one, that clients will seek the same in law firms—that the biggest practices with the most extensive network of local offices will claim those clients seeking uniform representation wherever their business takes them. As the theory goes, a Miami-based manufacturer with plants in New York and Los Angeles will move its business from a Florida-bound firm to a national outfit (read "Finley, Kumble") that can handle its needs in all three locations.

■ The first two strategies, lateral recruiting and national branching, serve as a foundation for the third: cross-selling. With specialized practice units woven through a network of offices, Finley, Kumble has multiple opportunities to land clients and to sell them once they are in the fold. Each service, each office, becomes both a client magnet and a profit center generating internal growth that multiplies exponentially with the size of the firm.

It works this way: antitrust laterals recruited ostensibly to serve New York clients are escorted on a grand tour of Finley offices where they are introduced to other clients known to be in the market for antitrust services. In Los Angeles, for example, the partner in charge informs a client how convenient it would be for Finley, Kumble—which already handles its real estate work—to add antitrust to its case load. Once inside the marketing grid, the client is sold again and again, this time to partners in the securities and general corporate practices. The opportunities are unlimited.

Underlying these strategies are two critical observations, call them "Kumbleisms," on which all of the firm's market plans are based:

> **KUMBLEISM ONE:** Small to midsized legal practices are an endangered species.

As corporate legal work available to the outside law firms is limited, increasingly, to narrow specialties (the bulk is handled in-house), the second-tier* firms, because they are weakest in the specialized practices, will have to struggle to survive.

Kumble is acutely aware that such Darwinian selection has brought profound change to the accounting profession, prompting hundreds of small CPA firms to seek refuge—through mergers—in the Big Eight giants that were once their competitors. And he has played to this survival instinct, employing it as the trump card in Finley, Kumble's merger strategy. Aware that the senior partners in modest-sized law firms, much like their counterparts in CPA land, see themselves being squeezed out of the market, he proposes a merger and, with it, instant membership in a large, national organization capable of competing—and more important, of surviving. Strength in numbers: Kumble has built the firm on this concept.

> **KUMBLEISM TWO:** Clients hire lawyers first, law firms second.

This, which Kumble calls "my secret code," reflects his conviction that talented lawyers jumping laterally from one firm to another take clients with them as they move to the highest bidder.

---

*"Second-tier" refers to those corporate law firms with from 50 to 200 lawyers.

"Lawyers bring in clients," Kumble says, "and law firms service them. I don't care what anyone says about a firm's history or traditions or any such nonsense. Except for a few clients who are still deep in the stone age, you don't get hired that way. Clients go with the lawyer they know, the lawyer they've worked with, the lawyer who delivers for them regardless of his firm's place in the pecking order. Sure you have to be able to service that client once he's on board, but it's the individual who gets him there.

"Those who fail to see this—and thank heaven there are many of them—overrate the power of the firm and underrate the power of the lawyers that make it work."

Belief in this "secret code" enables Kumble to turn a deaf ear to the controversy that surrounds his firm. That competitors delight in poisoning Finley, Kumble's reputation, that partners at megafirm rivals Skadden, Arps and Jones, Day pass black rumors of its imminent demise, and even that the *American Lawyer* paints a negative portrait of the firm and its name partners, are of only passing concern to the managing partner. Legal gossip, he believes, is of interest only to lawyers, academics, and journalists, none of whom hire law firms. A rich inventory of rainmakers—coupled with a wide sweep of practice services—will, he insists, draw clients to Finley, Kumble regardless of what the press or the competition says.

At its essence, Steve Kumble's marketing strategy boils down to an age-old formula that is controversial only to those lawyers who—like kept women—have never had to worry where their next dollar was coming from. Put simply, it is to find out what clients want—what they will pay for—and to use every means at your disposal to get that, and only that, to them. If this violates some irrelevant notion of right or wrong, if it diminishes collegiality, if it means one partner outearns another—all this is meaningless to the managing partner and the system he has created. Always Finley, Kumble does what is best for business. For a business that happens to be practicing law.

This was very much on Steve Kumble's mind as he reached into the dowdy Wall Street firm of Mudge, Rose, Guthrie, Alexander & Ferdon (best known as the partnership that once counted Richard Nixon among its top rainmakers), tapping Jim Normile, a senior associate in the firm's highly regarded and highly profitable municipal bond practice to lateral over to FK. With muni financings reaching record levels (as state governments were forced to finance projects abandoned by federal cutbacks) and legal fees rising in tandem, Kumble—whose built-in divining rod vibrates wildly at the first hint of emerging opportunities—was eager to add municipal finance to the firm's menu of services.

Stymied in his attempt to land a lateral partner from those firms with well-established muni practices (the big rainmakers were either put off by FK's image or unwilling to start a practice from scratch), Kumble found the ideal candidate in Normile, a Fordham Law School class of '76 graduate whose anemic appearance belies a fiery ambition that suffered under Mudge, Rose's lockstep handcuffs and that sought greater challenge elsewhere.

"I was in my fifth year with Mudge, making $65,000 at the time, when I got the indication—as associates do—that I would eventually make partner," Normile recalls. "Naturally I was exhilarated, but only until I heard what a Mudge, Rose partnership would really mean. The generous fellows were going to raise my income to $80,000, $5,000 of which would be subtracted for a capital contribution. So my grand elevation from associate to partner would be worth a lousy $10,000. Considering that *associates* at many of the best firms were making substantially more than I'd be making as a Mudge, Rose *partner*, the offer was one I could afford to pass up. I had no intention of waiting around for the 'big event.'

"The way I saw it, Mudge's problems were twofold. In the firm's heyday, when Nixon was there, they'd made a lot of partners in the corporate practice. And why not? With a full plate of work, there was enough money to keep everyone happy.

"But the times caught up with Mudge. Reflecting the trend throughout the profession, clients shifted more and more work in-house. The loss of business hit especially hard in the corporate practice—yes, the same practice where Mudge had made all those new partners. Soon, the place was crowded with $175,000- to $200,000-a-year guys without enough work to justify that kind of income. So, as is often the case with lockstep, the associates and the junior partners had to carry the weight. I didn't want any part of that."

Signing on with Finley, Kumble as a full partner—claiming a 50 percent increase over his Mudge, Rose salary—Normile was charged with building a department around his specialty and, in the process, making his new firm a factor in the municipal finance practice. That he had no management experience seemed of little consequence to Steve Kumble. That he thought like a businessman, like a marketer, was paramount.

"I never dwell much on the managing side of law," says Normile, a soft-spoken 33-year-old whose pale complexion is so light it appears to blend seamlessly with his white shirt. "Not because I don't want to, but because I don't think there's that much to it. All you have to do is keep enough business coming through the doors to keep your lawyers busy, and keep reminding those same lawyers that they have to satisfy their clients. Get the business. Serve it well. That's my definition of good management."

Ask giant law firm managing partners what they think of Finley, Kumble and to a man they claim they don't understand the firm—that this merged collage of seemingly eclectic legal practices leaves them baffled. But it's really as simple as Normile's management credo: get the business and serve it well. Precisely because it is devoid of mystique, FK is an enigma to all who've spent their careers in traditional firms.

In building his new practice, Kumble figured to "get the business" by trading on the weaknesses he perceived in established muni firms. Because the practice is transactional—with law firms hired by bond underwriters on a per deal basis rather than as permanent counsel— he knew that clients, especially investment bankers, would be willing to give the newcomers a chance to prove their mettle. Double the odds if the incumbents had fallen into "the trap of complacency."

"Some of the old names on Wall Street have grown up with a padlock on their markets," Normile says. "As a result, they've become lazy, unresponsive, arrogant. This is reflected in their client relationships. They work in a familiar pattern. When they first get the business, they carry the client around on their shoulders. No request is too great. It's the old 'your wish is my command' routine laid on really thick. But once the business is in the bank—once that client is up on the shelf with the other trophies—it's taken for granted and the relationship quickly deteriorates.

"At first, partners are dispatched to do the deals, then senior associates, then junior staffers who may be in over their heads. Every time the client needs assistance, a different lawyer is assigned to service him. So he sees a revolving cast of characters. There's no continuity— no opportunity to cement intimate client-lawyer relationships.

"Companies approaching the bloated law firms won't even be considered as clients unless they have the resources to assure substantial fees from the outset. The partners there live in a make-believe world where everything is supposed to be guaranteed. Risk is not in their vocabularies.

"Just how haughty, how deluded with grandeur the old firms can be really struck me during my Mudge days. On one occasion an accountant friend tipped me off to a prominent industrialist then in the market for a law firm to represent a new venture he'd formed in the alternative energy business. From the sound of it, the project appeared to have great potential, so I set up a meeting with the entrepreneur and two of our senior corporate partners. We gathered in a small conference room where the businessman, a real electric speaker, spelled out his business plan and ruminated about the kinds of legal work he would need.

"But the very instant he finished speaking—probably before he'd sounded the final syllable—one of the Mudge, Rose partners abruptly informed him that 'if you want us to work with you, we'll need a check for $25,000 before we'll go any further.' Well, my God, I felt this small. I'd invited the man to the meeting only to have him insulted by some Mudge partners who were 20 years behind the times. By their actions they were saying, 'We don't need you. We don't need anyone. Want to be a client here, you do things our way or you don't do them at all.' Well, I'm sorry but you can't do business that way anymore —not if you want to be a player in this profession."

To make Finley, Kumble a player in the municipal finance practice, Normile had first to negotiate the formidable challenge of listing his fledgling operation in the "Red Book,"* a Who's Who of the bond business that lists all of the lawyers and underwriters active in the field. Without this critical listing—which amounts to accreditation of the firm's bond practice—FK's bond opinions would not be accepted by potential clients.

But in a classic Catch 22, Red Book listings are limited to those law firms that have completed at least one bond deal. Fledgling practices, like Normile's, are effectively screened out: without a listing they cannot compete for business; without business they cannot qualify for a listing.

---

*Bond Buyer's Directory of Municipal Bond Dealers in the United States.

Or so it seemed. But Normile quickly showed his Finley, Kumble colors, combining naked opportunism with marketing prowess to break the deadlock. Leaning on a friend, whose Oklahoma law firm represented an industrial development agency in that state, Normile effectively borrowed the client for a single deal, just enough to qualify for inclusion in the Red Book. Within two months of joining the law's reigning scapegoat, the Mudge, Rose defector had managed to legitimize his still nascent practice, confirming Steve Kumble's faith in him and in the firm's ability to crack this lucrative market.

With the muni practice now officially part of Finley, Kumble's repertoire, it was rapidly integrated into the national organization, touted to partners across the branch network, and, in the firm's patented process, instantly cross-sold to clients. At a time when Normile might expect to be beating the bushes for business, the firm's internal sales machine took over, producing, in one major coup, the District of Columbia as a bond client. Already associated with Finley, Kumble's D.C. office (it was represented by star partner Robert Washington), the District appointed the firm as counsel for a $100 million housing bond. The practice was on its way.

Guided by mentor Steve Kumble—who gave his newest partner a crash course in the Finley, Kumble system—Normile turned from one intrafirm contact to another, always capitalizing on Finley, Kumble's resources and contacts. When the time came to invade Wall Street— where a law firm must be successful if it is to make it in municipal finance—the former Mudge, Roser reached out for assistance from Finley's reigning aristocracy, its premier rainmakers.

"I realized I could go it alone with the underwriters or I could go with some really heavy artillery," Normile says, the corner of his mouth turning upward in a sly, satisfied smile. "That's the strength of this firm. People say we're not cohesive but that's based on ignorance rather than a knowledge of how we operate. The fact is there are an awful lot of prominent and powerful lawyers here, all of whom pull together for the good of the firm. Let them know you need them and they're available. It worked that way with Carey."

As in former governor of New York Hugh L. Carey, a Finley, Kumble partner since 1983.* Famous, gregarious, larger than life, this sometime politician, sometime social butterfly proved the ideal em-

---

*The year after he left office.

issary to accompany the ghostly Mr. Normile on his marketing forays. As one of the few pols with credibility on Wall Street, the man had clout. He could deliver votes.

"Because he'd guided New York through its fiscal crisis and because he'd been through a thicket of municipal finance issues, he'd gained the respect of the investment bankers—a group we had to win over if we were going to make the practice successful," Normile says. "And I must admit that although I knew these people from my Mudge days and although I prided myself on having some influence with them, Carey's presence made an enormous impression. When we pitched firms like L. F. Rothschild, I could tell in the midst of our negotiations that we were winning them over as clients because of their affinity for the Governor."

Like Steve Kumble, Normile has come to believe that clients will turn to Finley, Kumble regardless of the firm's controversial image. Remember the "secret code": clients hire lawyers, not law firms. "The only ones who give a shit about what's said in the legal press are other lawyers and they don't pay the bills," Normile snaps. "Clients couldn't care less."

While there are exceptions, this is essentially true. More and more in today's legal marketplace, the client in search of counsel hires the lawyer best suited to do the job regardless of his affiliation. Just a decade ago, the notion of a crude upstart test-marketing a new practice on the likes of Morgan Stanley, First Boston, and Goldman Sachs—and in the process taking business from established law firms—would be unthinkable. But Finley, Kumble claimed all three while the ink was still wet on its Red Book listing.

The truth is, Finley, Kumble has detected a change in the market—in the "code" for hiring lawyers—that others have resisted or simply chosen to ignore. Asked about her decision to hire Finley as bond counsel, a First Boston vice president echoes Kumbleisms as if the man behind them wrote her lines.

"This business feeds on rumor, innuendo, muck, dirt, assorted scandals of every kind. Do something wrong, something that appears wrong, something that others want to appear wrong, and everyone on Wall Street knows about it before the closing bell.

"So of course I'd heard the rap against Finley, Kumble. That it is not—how shall I say it—among the classier law firms. But I didn't concern myself with that. More important to me was that Jim Normile came highly recommended from First Boston sources and other contacts I trusted on the Street. I hire lawyers, not law firms, and it appeared quite clear to me that Normile had the qualifications to serve us well.

"Two factors figure into my hiring decisions: fees—they can't be off-the-wall exorbitant—and the lawyer's reputation. Finley, Kumble scored well on both counts. That's all that matters. Failing to hire them because of some silly professional feud is, I think, rather dumb."

Just the kind of talk that makes the legal mummies unravel in their cases. No doubt, Finley, Kumble's lateral-transfer practice-building system appears to be an unqualified success. In two years, for example, the municipal bond practice has completed 90 financings worth more than $5 billion and has grown from a single professional to three partners and 13 associates based in New York, Los Angeles, and Washington, D.C. But critics say that the picture is misleading. That Finley, Kumble, for all of its dramatic growth, is less a large law firm than a tenuous association of wildly disparate lawyers united only in their quest for the fast buck. And that instead of being a strength, Finley's lack of tradition will lead ultimately to its destruction.

"They do it all with mirrors," says a senior partner with Jones, Day, Reavis & Pogue, a Cleveland-based megafirm with a dramatically different approach to national practice. "From a distance, it looks like they have it all—the offices, the talent, the business systems. But get up close and you recognize it's a mirage—that the whole apparatus is fine-tuned to bring in clients with hardly a thought to serving them once they're lured into the web. Can you sustain a practice on that basis? Consider me doubtful, highly doubtful. Finley, Kumble's not the big-league law firm it thinks it is—or, more important, that it wants everyone else to think it is. What you have there is one hell of an optical illusion."

Mudge, Rose name partner Robert Ferdon echoes this charge, holding that for all its talk of instant status in the bond market, Finley, Kumble is still a petty player.

"They may represent this or that investment banker on this or that transaction, but I wouldn't read all that much into that if I were you. Underwriters seed their business all over the place. Each one of them uses eight, ten, maybe more law firms as bond counsel. It's a transactional, deal-by-deal practice.

"The more enduring relationships are established with the issuing agencies, and here Finley, Kumble has come up short. To my knowledge, they haven't made any substantial inroads with these really critical clients. And unlike the firms that are legitimate forces in this practice, you don't see Finley, Kumble doing anything significant on the national level. What little work they have is centered in New York.''

Ferdon's swipe at FK goes even further, insinuating—as is the widespread perception—that Finley, Kumble is heavy with prima donnas more comfortable in a PR agency than a court of law.

"In the past five years, bond practice has become embroiled in a thicket of complex tax issues. It's a real difficult area of the law— one that requires highly trained, highly experienced lawyers who've spent time down in the trenches learning how to get deals done. Does Finley, Kumble measure up? Let me put it this way. You can't do justice to this business with a bunch of front men bringing in the clients if there's no one of substance to take over once they're through the door.

"Yes, Finley, Kumble has the former governor of New York, but we have Judah Gribetz, Carey's chief counsel for his first four years in office and as far as I'm concerned the real brains behind the operation. He's not a politician, but that's not what clients need. He's a superb lawyer. You tell me which is more valuable.''

Ferdon also refutes Normile's claim about the alleged decline of Mudge's corporate practice—("business is very strong," he says) and denies Normile's assertion that he was destined for Mudge, Rose partnership.

"Mr. Normile was never told he'd be made a partner, and it's far from certain that would have occurred had he remained with us. Partnership appointments, made by a vote of the firm, must be preceded by a recommendation of the executive committee, an action it never took on Mr. Normile's behalf. He did credible work here but that's about as far as it went.''

Just how Normile would have fared at Mudge, Rose will never be known. But that he left an established muni practice for a makeshift setup without a single client to call its own—this, critics say, reveals a dangerous flaw lurking deep in the bowels of Finley, Kumble.

"What happens when the music stops?" asks Jones, Day's managing partner Dick Pogue. "I'll be pleased to answer that. When you've assembled a collection of lawyers who have joined a firm not for the joy of practicing law together but solely because that firm bids highest for their services, they'll depart as soon as business declines and the money is better elsewhere. Because there's no loyalty, no collegiality, the firm will come unglued. I hate to dignify that kind of thing with the designation of 'law firm.' "

The prevalent knock against Finley, Kumble: that it is actually a federation of sole practitioners masquerading as a law firm. Says a partner at Chicago-based Sidley & Austin, a bastion of traditional legal values:

"Finley, Kumble's a revolving door. I call it Kumble & Goin. A lot of the guys there have ricocheted, like pinballs, from one firm to another. Just tell them who's offering the sweetest deal at any given time and they grab a plane in that direction.

"What's wrong with that? One thing is wrong, terminally wrong. When your people are here today, gone tomorrow—when they lack the pride and tradition that comes only with time—then you've got little more than a bunch of free-lance lawyers who happen to share the same letterhead.

"When they see this, when they recognize Kumble & Goin for what it is, substantial clients won't want any part of it. To a major corporation—itself a continuing entity—the quality of a law firm is of more importance than the quality of any one individual who practices in it. Client management is astute enough to recognize that lawyers are transient—they die, retire, or depart for any number of reasons— but a firm's traditions, the guidelines under which its lawyers practice, remain constant."

Thus the essential clash between Finley, Kumble's "cult of the individual" and the mainstream practitioners' "ode to the institution." The difference makes for a violent contrast in management philosophy: at Finley, the individual is leveraged to enhance and enrich the firm; at the others, this is reversed. This, Kumble insists, plays right into his hands, assuring FK of a steady stream of bright and ambitious defectors.

"When lawyers move laterally to our side of the street, the abandoned firms chalk it up to some kind of voodoo on our part. But it's really nothing more than our willingness to recognize the contribution individuals can make to the profitability of a law firm and to reward those people accordingly.

"Why should a star allow himself to be buried alive in an institution that's got his whole life, his whole career, predetermined regardless of his performance? Why should he tolerate lockstep when it shifts a firm's assets away from its most dynamic members, rewarding instead those who are least productive? The answer, of course, is that he shouldn't. Not when he can go to a firm with incentive compensation that will reward him for his contribution regardless of his age or his years of service.

"Not everyone is capable of being a star. But those who are should be compensated for it."

An article of religious faith at Finley, Kumble, which functions, more than any other law firm, as a pure meritocracy. Unlike the lockstep firms, whose earnings curves are marked by a gradual elevation from junior to senior partners, Finley's reveals a staggering disparity between those journeyman partners without a significant client following, who earn as little as $100,000, to the million-a-year rainmakers. Further evidence, critics say, of a firm built on salesmanship rather than scholarly achievement—and of a partnership held together with a watery glue that will wash away at the first sign of adversity.

Kumble responds on two levels, charging first that he is attacked not so much for what he does but for being the first to do it, and second, that all firms, even the holier-than-thou Shearmans and Milbanks, are glued together by crass and commercial economics.

"We challenged traditions, and that always upsets those who are protected by traditions and who are afraid to compete without them. But most of the other firms have been forced to follow our lead. There's hardly a partnership today that hasn't modified lockstep or isn't considering such a move. Nor are there firms that won't contemplate lateral hires or branch offices.

"I just read in this week's *National Law Journal* that Weil, Gotshal is opening up in Dallas. How? By hiring a select group of graduates from Texas law schools, grooming them as associates, and then eight years later making them partners? Hell no. They rounded up a bunch of laterals from Dallas firms, stuck them together in an office, and called it Weil, Gotshal. Just the kind of thing everyone points fingers at us for doing.

"I'm not saying that some firms don't have stronger glue than ours. Nor am I saying that if we cease to be profitable, people won't leave. But I am saying that they'd leave all the other firms just as quickly.

"Many of the laterals we've hired have come from firms with all the trappings of history and tradition, where the glue was supposedly rock hard. They came because we offered them more—because at a certain dollar figure (and almost everyone has his price) the glue became less important than the lawyer's personal financial goals. The fact is that the notion of collegial partners puffing on their pipes and quietly going to their graves in a dying firm is a myth. I don't know of any business organization in the world that can hold on to people forever when it's clear they can do better elsewhere.

"There's no such glue known to man."

Kumble's point is that collegiality, the stick so often used to batter the more aggressive firms, is a by-product of success rather than of some mystical allegiance to the institution or its founders. Where the partners feel a strong sense of loyalty to their firms and to each other, it is because they are prospering, and in many cases getting rich together. Should this earnings streak abruptly end, collegiality will suffer along with the balance sheet. When New York's Donovan, Leisure, Newton & Irvine, once a temple of collegiality, suffered through a difficult period—precipitated by the loss of megaclient Eastman Kodak—many of its lawyers lateraled out to greener pastures. Glue or no glue.

Making money, Kumble believes, will prevent this, bonding the partners to each other and to the firm regardless of its traditions or lack of them.

Finley, Kumble has risen to the ranks of the giants by replacing the traditional emphasis on mystique with the three cornerstones of effective marketing: distribution, inventory, and service. As managing partner and resident visionary, Steve Kumble has been the driving force in the marketplace, expanding FK's presence in key cities, staffing the branch offices with marketable talents, and creating high-profile practice boutiques. All with the singular objective of creating the dominant law firm in the United States.

Throughout the building process, Kumble's efforts have hinged on his ability to develop a national network of offices that functions as a single firm rather than a hodgepodge of warring factions. But here too the firm has come away with a puffy black eye. As a firm possessed of a master plan—a firm in a desperate rush to make its mark in the profession—it has exported its brand of legal practice across the map.

With every merger, every lateral entry, critics say, has come a dilution of the firm's essential character, as new partners and new associates with new clients and new thoughts on the practice of law have entered the fold.

"What does the name Finley, Kumble mean?" asks a partner at Davis Polk. "Even Steve Kumble doesn't know. He can't, because it means one thing in Los Angeles where real estate golden boy Marshall Manley holds forth and another in Washington, D.C., where former Senator Joe Tydings hangs his hat. They're both Finley, Kumble partners but they're as different as day and night, and I'll bet they have nothing to do with one another minus occasional client referrals, which, considering that's what their firm is all about, shouldn't be very surprising."

He may have a point. While the honorable Mr. Tydings, a stylish and charming southern gentleman given to vanilla white suits and blushing red ties, insists (as if he'd been programmed by the men from Manhattan) that his office is at one with Finley's outposts in Los Angeles, New York, and Miami, he often slips up (Freudian or not), referring to Manley's operation as the California "firm." Writing this off to a "poor choice of words," he appears, however, to view Finley, Kumble as less a singular body than the party line insists it is.

"On paper, mergers look so easy you wonder why everyone doesn't do them routinely," says one management partner with a big New York law firm. "It looks like such an obvious shortcut to building your practice, adding on clients and so on. But anyone who's ever explored mergers closely and objectively knows that they're a management riddle. Just how to incorporate what are essentially different firms with different traditions, cultures, and personalities into a homogeneous unit has yet, at least from this man's perspective, to be answered. Any product of mergers that I've yet seen has suffered quality of practice problems. The managing partners sitting in New York or Chicago or Cleveland just cannot assure their clients that the quality they'll get from other lawyers in their firms is the same as from those who've grown up with them in the same culture. No booklets on practice standards can make up for the patchwork of quality standards that run through firms stitched together by businessmen."

Much as he denies it—and he does so vehemently—Steve Kumble seems bored to tears with the quality issue, preferring instead to concentrate on those things that go in and out of a Texas Instruments calculator. The quintessential numbers cruncher, he appears to gauge mergers primarily for the impact they will have on the partners' paychecks.

This apparent myopia has led to embarrassing incidents. Consider the episode involving co-managing partner Marshall Manley's efforts to establish an Orange County office by merging with the five-month-old law firm of Kray, Newmeyer, Landrum & Dillion. Soon after Manley negotiated a deal (May 1984) with partner Steven Kray (whose firm became part of Finley, Kumble), Kray's three partners—all in the young to middle thirties—cried foul, claiming the deal was done behind their backs.

They had good reason to complain. Under the terms of the deal, Kray would join Finley, Kumble as a partner while his former partners at Kray, Newmeyer, Landrum & Dillion would be demoted to Finley, Kumble associates. For his part, Kray insisted that he acted according to an oral agreement granting him the authority to structure a merger unilaterally, but the others denied this. They left to start their own firm ten weeks after the merger was complete.

"I was the only equity partner," Kray says, referring to the structure at Kray, Newmeyer, Landrum & Dillion. "The others were partners in name only. Because I had total voting control, I could structure any deal I wanted."

Tom Newmeyer, his former partner, denies this.

"We always held ourselves as equal partners, internally and to the world. And even in the merger agreement with Finley, Kumble—which Kray tried to conceal from us—our firm was described as a partnership in good standing."

Manley, who attributes the departure of the associates to financial differences they had with Kray before the merger, contends that their loss was not material to Finley, Kumble.

"Our only objective was to get Steve Kray into the firm to anchor the Orange County office. There's nothing we didn't know about his firm that we should have known."

But Steve Kumble, who rarely challenges his fair-haired West Coast rainmaker (Manley* is reported to bring in $9 million of the firm's

---

*Whether or not the Orange County office was opened as tactfully as possible is open to question, but there is no doubt that Manley has since built it into a thriving practice.

roughly $125 million in annual fees), admits that "we fucked up on that one. Initially, we'd planned to open our own Orange County office. But after acquiring the necessary space, we decided to postpone our plans and wound up subletting the space to that other firm, what's their name? Kray, someone and someone. Some time after, I forget how long, the idea came up to merge Mr. Kray's firm into ours. Because he's a dynamic guy, very capable in the estates and trusts area that we wanted to build up in that market, the merger idea sounded attractive.

"But—but it seemed that Kray and his people hadn't reconciled their own financial differences. Maybe the guys we were talking to weren't talking for everyone. And maybe we should have known that."

Asked if Manley was responsible for the apparent lack of information, Kumble, ordinarily a paragon of cool, fidgets nervously in his seat.

"Well, ah, ah, several people were involved in that deal. Marshall did meet with the principal, but he had no way of knowing about the problems between the partners."

Forget the excuses; Finley, Kumble was taken by surprise. In negotiating the Orange County deal, the national megafirm apparently never bothered to learn enough about its newest target to know that three of the four name partners would object to the agreement.

"I never met with anyone from Finley, Kumble until after they signed a deal with Kray," Newmeyer says. "They were hiring me without knowing who or what I was."

Unacquainted with three quarters of the firm's principals, what could Finley have known about Kray, Newmeyer's legal skills, standards of practice—the elements, it seems, that a national firm concerned with uniform quality would investigate first?

The episode gives some credence to the rap that Finley, Kumble is hell bent on mergers; that it pursues growth for growth's sake. Steve Kumble, who's heard it all more times than he cares to admit, dismisses the charges as the petty jealousies of weak and worried competitors. And while there is some truth to this (surely the declining firms are threatened by this aggressive upstart) there is more here than jealous backbiting. Skadden, Arps's Peter Mullen, Jones, Day's Dick Pogue, Sidley & Austin's Howard Trienens—all prominent partners in firms more successful than Finley, Kumble—have no reason to be jealous. So why do they belittle FK? Why do they speak disparagingly about the "house of cards" Kumble built? Why do they care what Steve Kumble is after and how he goes about achieving it?

The answer reverts back to debate between those who see the practice of law as a profession first and a business second and those who prefer to reverse that order of priorities. While the two sides clash on this issue, most are willing to accept their adversaries as reasonable men and women given to different points of view.

That courtesy is not always extended to Steve Kumble. Because he is perceived by some as a businessman in lawyer's clothing, as an entrepreneur whose methodology in the legal market is all too similar to Ray Kroc's in the hamburger business, he is considered an outsider whose aggressive tactics threaten the very professionalism that lawyers —even those at the vanguard of modern practice—pride themselves on. Even the most ambitious and commercially sensitive practitioners distinguish themselves, on the basis of this professionalism, from their corporate clients, holding it as both a source of pride and an asset convertible into substantial fees. Only by retaining the distinction between professionals and businessmen, it is believed, can lawyers bring something unique to the marketplace and at the same time retain their image of indispensability.

Because Kumble is seen by some as clouding this distinction— because they believe that he fails to temper business decisions with long-standing professional considerations—they dislike him. The picture is painted of a lateral-transfer and merger addict who has assembled a sloppy collection of disconnected legal practices into the McDonald's of law.

But as the megafirm managing partner the others love to hate most and as the whipping boy of the legal press, Steve Kumble is often underestimated both as a lawyer and a businessman. While competitors delight in recounting war stories of his deals gone awry and while the press feeds on embarrassments like the Orange County fiasco, most of his major deals—like the merger with the Washington, D.C., law firm of Danzansky, Dickey, Tydings, Quint & Gordon—have met the acid test of successful mergers, creating a combined entity that has proved to be greater than the sum of its parts. For all who consider Finley, Kumble an enigma, the behind-the-scenes machinations of this 1981 merger reveal how and why the firm operates as it does.

Beginning in the late 1970s, something started bothering Steve Kumble. A minor annoyance at first, it quickly escalated to a full-fledged migraine.

The cause of this malaise was none other than a glaring gap in Finley, Kumble's practice grid. Increasingly, clients were demanding that legal matters pending before any arm, agency, or branch of the federal government be handled not by Finley, Kumble's shuttle-hopping New York partners (as the headache-plagued Kumble preferred), but instead by one of the indigenous D.C. firms viewed as the high priests of Washington practice. Experienced in the arcane world of the regulatory commissions (SEC, FTC, FCC, ICC), old capital hands such as Covington & Burling and Arnold & Porter had carved out a rich and protected practice that for years drew lucrative referral business from most of the nation's leading law firms.

As competition intensified in the legal profession and as the Washington practices grew in tandem with the increasing government regulation of American business, law firms, even those without national ambitions, began to open D.C. branches. As a result, those without Washington representation—Finley, Kumble among them—began to view the tradition of D.C. referrals as "client leakage." In effect, they now were handing over Washington referrals to firms that competed with them in other cities.

In a typical case, a Finley, Kumble client prominent in the financial services business found itself embroiled in a Securities and Exchange Commission enforcement proceeding. Recognizing the particular savvy of the Washington practices in SEC matters, management asked FK to arrange for a D.C. firm to captain the case. Hoping to prevent this "leakage," Kumble suggested instead that one of his New York partners, a former SEC staff attorney, service the client from FK's headquarters.

But in the end the client balked, insisting, in so many words, that Finley refer the work to a firm with a D.C. office, or else. . . . Without a local practice of its own, Finley Kumble had no choice but to farm out the case. But the managing partner made a mental note to close the gap.

Kumble explored several options for creating a D.C. presence:

- Dispatch a landing party of New York partners to secure a beachhead in the nation's capital. Appealing because it could utilize Finley, Kumble's political connections and the contingent of Manhattan-based lawyers with previous experience in Washington law, the option was nevertheless dismissed as undoable on the grounds that Washington could not be cracked from the outside in.

"You're talking about a political Peyton Place," says a partner with the Washington law firm of Crowell & Moring. "Here, power stems from who you know much more than what you know. And those who-you-knows have to be cultivated over many years. An outside firm can't simply storm this place with a bunch of brilliant Harvard boys and hope to make an impact here. The names on your Rolodex are more important than technical knowledge. Clients know that. That's why to open shop here successfully—to gain some meaningful business—you've got to be a factor in this community, or at least get married to someone who is."

■ Tap directly into the politico-legal circuit by recruiting a prominent government official—say the chairman of the FCC or an SEC commissioner—installing him as a Finley, Kumble partner, and framing him with a supporting cast of experienced laterals.

But this too had an inherent weakness. As Finley later learned in an abortive attempt to establish a Miami presence on the shoulders of a local rainmaker, few lawyers are cut out to manage practices. Bureaucrats are especially poor choices. The former commissioner might well bring in clients, but could he run the practice? The odds were against it.

As the list of options grew shorter, Kumble and other name partners began to view a merger as the only viable strategy. But this too proved problematic. Finding a sizeable and reputable DC practice willing to merge with a New York firm whose name was mud in some quarters of the profession took some searching and sweet talking, courting and convincing. Word has it that on a number of occasions FK's merger overtures were rebuffed; on others, Kumble found the merger candidates unacceptable. But then a chance meeting between Kumble and former U.S. Senator from Maryland Joseph Tydings, then managing partner of the D.C. law firm of Danzansky, Dickey, Tydings, Quint & Gordon, led to the deal Kumble was looking for.

The two managing partners first met when Kumble's wife Margaret*—a prominent thoroughbred breeder–syndicator and a major FK client—asked her husband to accompany her to the Laurel International, a thoroughbred event sponsored by Tydings's brother-in-law John D. Shapiro.

"Although we met at a social event, we found ourselves talking shop from the start," Kumble recalls. "At first it was real banal stuff. You know, how's your firm, how's mine, how's the weather—that kind of thing. But with the small talk out of the way, the conversation turned to some serious issues, and before I knew exactly what was happening, I was standing there with a drink in my hand pitching a merger deal.

"Even more surprising—because I thought it was such a long shot—Tydings appeared captivated by the idea. So I kept talking, selling, citing Finley, Kumble's impressive growth record, naming some of our more prominent partners, reeling off a few of our better-known clients. All the time, he just listens. Not a word passes from his lips. I figure the guy's too mesmerized to talk.

"Finally, I end my monologue and look to Tydings for a reaction. But there is none. It's then that I realize—to my chagrin—that he hadn't the slightest interest in what I was saying. What I'd mistaken for interest was actually indifference, boredom, whatever. The point is, he didn't care a whit for my proposal."

All the more challenge for Kumble. While an old granddad of the profession might have viewed Tydings's coolness as a rebuke to his firm—which in part it may have been—Kumble pressed forward, cajoling, romancing, employing every technique at his disposal to interest the former Senator and other key Danzansky, Dickey partners in a merger.

His strategy, one used successfully in any number of FK mergers, was to focus more on the dangers of independent practice than on the benefits of combined operations. The objective: to make the merger target, in this case Danzansky, Dickey, aware of its vulnerability in the midsector of the legal marketplace. This accomplished, Kumble's message—and the sales pitch that went with it—began to sink in. Faced with the specter of outside law firms from major business centers

---

*She operates under the professional name of Peggy Vandervort.

throughout the nation opening Washington offices of their own (to keep the government-related work in-house), the Danzansky, Dickey partners began to see the merits of a national affiliation. Minus the cachet of a Covington & Burling or an Arnold & Porter, Danzansky, Dickey (much like other independent D.C. specialists) would suffer a precipitous decline as former referral partners moved on to the already crowded Washington turf. By joining the FK network, Danzansky, Dickey would be assured a steady flow of business as Kumble's multi-city cross-selling grid directed clients to its doors.

But not all the Danzansky partners saw it this way. Some, fearing the loss of collegiality and local control that a merger would bring, resisted the move. According to a source privy to the negotiations, the opposition argued that the firm should remain independent and complained furthermore that Finley, Kumble's shabby reputation made it an improper suitor. "To back up this charge," the source recalls, "one of the opponents announced that he'd learned from friends at New York's Willkie, Farr & Gallagher that Finley, Kumble was not considered a quality firm. That it was the poor relation of New York's legal community.

"Naturally the partners were concerned about this—no one wanted another firm's stains to rub off on Danzansky, Dickey—so some of the guys called contacts of their own to learn just how much weight the charges carried. When everyone shared their notes, the consensus was that Finley, Kumble—in spite of a less than glowing reputation with other lawyers and the press—got uniformly high marks from the ultimate arbiters of a law firm's fate, its clients.

"Putting Willkie, Farr's comments in the context of real-world New York legal politics, it was felt that any law firm that had grown from a handful of lawyers to about 150, as Finley had done at the time, had to have stepped on a lot of toes on the way up. So the attacks against the firm were taken with a grain of salt and rejected as sufficient reason to block the merger."

But there was another factor at work. Opponents of the merger faced a formidable opponent in their own managing partner. Although initially cool to the prospect of a Finley, Kumble merger (perhaps for fear of the same image problem that worried other partners), Tydings, more than his colleagues, recognized that Danzansky, Dickey would be in for rough sledding in D.C.'s increasingly competitive market and had come to the conclusion that the firm needed a strong ally even before the fateful meeting with Steve Kumble.

"In the period from 1971—the year I joined Danzansky after leaving the Senate—to 1979, I watched as damn near every law firm with more than 100 attorneys opened a Washington office," Tydings complains, hands clasped behind his head, legs sprawled across his desk. His woodsy, plaidy office—as much a museum of political mementos (including prominently displayed photos of John Kennedy, who appointed him U.S. Attorney for Maryland in 1961) as a work space—befits a former member of the world's most exclusive club. "How did the other firms get started here in Washington? Typically, they'd send over one or two partners from the home base, beef them up with a well-known lateral from the public sector—former commissioners were always popular—and then proceed to lose money just for the sake of telling their clients they had a Washington office. That the office was bathed in red ink was considered the price for holding on to those big clients who demanded a Washington presence. So these firms weren't leaving Washington no matter how poorly they did. They were here to stay.

"Well, only the blind would miss the handwriting on the wall. With the firms that traditionally referred their Washington business to you now competing for those same dollars—and with more and more of the firms going in that direction—our market had to be shrinking. Sooner or later, those firms that lived on Washington referrals alone would find themselves in dire straits. I didn't want Danzansky, Dickey to be included in that company. So I knew something had to be done, but exactly what that would be wasn't clear in mind.

"Not until I attended a legal seminar in the fall of 1978. Quite by accident, I was assigned to a workshop for the managing partners of large law firms. Once I realized the mistake, I intended, naturally, to go to the right session, but the discussions had already begun and I was captivated by the theme that was emerging.

"Speaker after speaker addressed what was then the novel concept of a 'national law firm.' I'd read snippets about this in the media but for the first time the whole picture came into focus, especially the fascinating part about funneling business through the various offices and practices within the same firm. As I stayed and listened throughout the session, I could see the opportunities clearer and clearer. Wow, could I see the opportunities. I left that place convinced that we needed a national affiliation.

"With this in mind, I went over to visit with Newton Minow, Sidley & Austin's managing partner, soon after they opened up in Washington. I indicated, in so many words, that we might be interested in joining up with them. Unfortunately—so I thought at the time—they indicated, in so many words, that with a Washington office of their own, they didn't need us. So much for that. They never followed up and neither did I.

"Once I had time to reflect on that meeting—which was more in the way of an informal discussion than official firm business—I recognized that we needed a merger mate that would benefit from a strong Washington practice as much as we would benefit from having a strong practice beyond Washington. So when the Finley, Kumble deal unfolded, it appeared tailor made for us. Once I did some homework, once Kumble, Heine, and Underberg came to Washington for additional talks and for get-acquainted sessions, I believed, very strongly, that a merger with Finley, Kumble would be of enormous benefit to both firms."

But another lurking problem threatened to bury the merger talks in the good-idea-that-never-worked-out column: Danzansky, Dickey's traditions prohibited mergers—seven previous merger proposals had been killed on this basis. Determined to change the rules and to authorize negotiations with Finley, Kumble, Tydings called a retreat, gathering the partners for a two-day session in Reston, Virginia.

The meeting was marked by bitterness, with the various factions —those for and against mergers in general and with Finley, Kumble specifically—battling it out on an emotional level. Tydings, the old pol, worked his partners the way he'd worked his Senate colleagues, flattering, threatening, twisting arms, calling in IOUs. As a substantial rainmaker and a notable whose name lent the firm a substantial asset in a town infatuated with personalities, he had influence, clout, brute power. When the dust cleared, a majority vote approved the merger but two of the opposition leaders chose to leave rather than join the new firm.

In February 1981, roughly a year after their chance meeting, Kumble, Tydings & Co. signed an agreement merging Danzansky, Dickey with the fast-growing FK. Viewed from both sides the merger made good business sense. By creating a Washington presence, it filled a glaring void in Finley, Kumble's practice grid, making the firm more attractive to clients demanding national representation. For Danzansky, Dickey, it stemmed the threatened loss of business and laid a pipeline for new clients.

Judging by the numbers, the deal has lived up to its promise. In the five years since the merger, Danzansky, Dickey has grown from 44 to 117 lawyers, with 60 percent of the increase attributed to internal growth.

Never bashful about his accomplishments—or for that matter what he fancies as his accomplishments while much of the world is still unsure—Kumble sums up the merger this way:

"We took what was always a first-rate Washington law firm—one that had been in business for 50 years before merging with Finley, Kumble—and gave it strengths and resources it did not have. Today, it is regarded as one of the premier practitioners in the D.C. legal community."

Not quite. Few outside the Finley, Kumble family appear to view the firm's Washington outpost as one of the capital's "premier practitioners." From all indications, it is seen as a respectable but lackluster shop that is several notches down the prestige curve from the Covingtons and the Arnold & Porters. Its practice, though steady and solid, rarely involves the landmark issues that lend the more prominent firms their special status.

"You have to remind yourself that the old Danzansky bunch practices in this town," says a partner with D.C.'s Crowell & Moring. "They don't exactly make the *Post* on a regular basis and you rarely bump up against them on major cases. They've always been at the fringe of Washington practice, before and after the merger with Finley, Kumble.

"There was some hope that would change when Tydings joined the firm after leaving the Senate. He was touted as a Kennedy intimate, which, in the glory days of that tribe, was thought to mean instant prestige and a good deal of business to go with it. But I don't think that ever lived up to its promise, and now that the bloom is off the Kennedy name, I can't see it being much of a bankable asset.

"Not to say that Tydings isn't a good lawyer with solid connections. Many top law firms in this town would want to add his name to the partnership. And that, in a nutshell, is Kumble's modus operandi, both here and throughout the country. He goes after a few big names—names he can market to clients—and if there's some chaff associated with the wheat, he accepts it as part of the package.

"What does he wind up with? A couple of superstars surrounded by a platoon of mediocre talent. That's why Finley, Kumble will never be ranked among the most distinguished law firms. Not in my opinion."

Finley, Kumble's place in the legal hierarchy may be irrelevant. That the Washington practice (as well as its other merger mates) is growing and prosperous and integrated into the cross-selling network is of greater import to the partners, especially Kumble, who deserves much of the credit for making the merger work. The secret to his success is not only in the way he structures deals, but in the way he builds on the foundation and massages the personalities so that the relationships work even if they do so more from raw ambition than good will and collegiality.

Contrary to popular opinion that he is simply a deal maker, Kumble's real strength is in his manipulative abilities. Because he recognizes the near-universal quest for power and money, he has been able to design a system that tames even the most raving egos, giving them the incentive to join his legal Luftwaffe and to perform once inside of it.

In making this work, he has based his leadership on a combination of power and persuasion, on innovation and insight. In many ways, he is Finley, Kumble.

The truth is that while virtually all major law firms (with the notable exception of Jones, Day, Reavis & Pogue, which prides itself as an aristocracy) give lip service to the democratic process, one or two key partners generally wield a lopsided share of the power. Write this in capital letters when the founding partner is still active. As the architect of the institution, he has built the firm from the ground up, piecing together the lawyers, the offices, the practice departments into a synergistic whole that, if the firm is successful, is greater than the sum of its parts. And he has done so according to a formula that, like the recipe for Coca-Cola, remains a well-kept secret.

"Steve started concocting his plan for Finley, Kumble from the firm's earliest days," says a law firm partner who has known and observed Kumble for years, "and he's still the only one who knows how the whole thing fits together.

"It's as if he has this little piece of paper in his pocket with a blueprint of how the firm is going to look. He knows which city is next on the hit list, how it will be staffed, what kind of lawyers will be needed, what kind of clients will be targeted. And he knows when and where the process will begin again.

"Sure, all of this is put to a vote, but it's difficult for anyone to challenge Steve because no one else is privy to that blueprint. No one else has as great a feel for how the various partners, especially the laterals, fit into the blueprint, how the various offices stand in the great scheme of things, and where the firm is ultimately headed. When one man has a clear vision—when he sees the forest while the others can't see over the trees—there's a natural tendency to defer to him on critical issues. That's where a guy like Kumble draws his strength."

Says Joe Tydings, "If we didn't have a Steve Kumble, we'd have to go out and invent one. You need a central figure to hold the pieces in place."

Not that the lead partners are willing to delegate all power to the creator of the Kumbleism. Heine, Underberg, Manley, Tydings, and Bob Washington are all experienced infighters, protective of their rank and position in the firm and unwilling to serve under a dictator. This is especially true of the key men outside the headquarters office, all of whom are sensitive to domination by the New Yorkers. In naming Manley as Finley, Kumble's co-managing partner in February 1984, the ruling clique (led, of course, by Kumble) was responding, in part, to the realization that a truly national law firm cannot be ruled entirely from New York.

"The way I understand it, Manley made it clear that he'd be less inclined to listen to competitive job offers—which, considering his extraordinary legal and rainmaking skills, probably come his way daily—if the West Coast practice shared in the power rather than being at the receiving end of it," says a partner at Skadden, Arps. "And his point was well taken. If Finley, Kumble—or our firm for that matter—is going to make a big stink about being a national practice, then hell, we've got to disperse some of the power beyond the East Side of Manhattan. Fail to integrate your key people into the decision-making process and they'll up and leave."

Though they give Kumble credit for his entrepreneurial skills and though they value his leadership for the impact it has on the bottom line and in turn on their partnership shares, the key men in the firm operate within a limited sphere of independence. Tydings, for example, has drawn a line around the D.C. office, a line he expects Kumble to respect. Consider this conversation between Tydings and the author:

MS: Steve Kumble says that if he identified a merger candidate in Washington, he could push through the merger even if this office objected. An unlikely scenario, he admits, but one within the realm of possibility.

JT: Not true.

MS: You mean he's wrong.

JT: He's dead wrong.

MS: You're saying there's something in the partnership agreements which prohibits a majority vote of the management committee from approving a D.C. merger over this office's objections?

JT: It just couldn't happen. Period.

MS: But why?

JT: Because we wouldn't let it.

MS: But what if they voted in favor of it and tried to force the merger in spite of your objections?

JT: We're too successful here—too important—for them to try that. They don't want to risk the good thing they have here.

MS: Meaning?

JT: I'm only going to say that it can't happen. If this is to be a truly national firm, the various offices must have a say in how it's run. I've gone to the mat with New York on this a number of times, and I'll do so again and again if need be.

In one particularly nasty confrontation—which the powers that be have since tried to sweep under the rug—Kumble tried to force the D.C. office to take on Joe Califano, Jr., former Secretary of HEW and a director of American Can Co. As a prominent Washington figure with substantial rainmaking credentials, Califano was the ideal candidate for Kumble's star-recruiting system. But Tydings, flexing his political biceps (he was then managing partner), objected. Whether this revealed his insecurity at having another name player join the ranks, is uncertain. But his opposition to Califano prevailed. Kumble had to accept the limits of his power.

"You need a guy like Steve to put a firm like this together and to keep it whole," Tydings says, repeating a favorite theme. "But it can't be a one-man band. Steve knows that. He knows it better than anyone else. He's built this firm—and he's built it right."

Whether Kumble's techniques are "right" for the legal profession will be the subject of debate for years to come. Clearly, the white-shoe crowd will continue to snub their noses at his "crass commercialism" for as long as they can bank on their inherited relationships. But whether he is doing "something right" for Finley, Kumble is easier to call. By all objective standards, building an eight-lawyer law firm into one of the nation's largest practices is a major accomplishment.

Like his counterparts in accounting, engineering, and architecture—men and women who have turned professional practices into major businesses—Kumble has recognized that professional training is poor preparation for a businessman-manager-entrepreneur. And he has forced himself to challenge the mind set that is the by-product of a legal education.

"You learn in law school to think logically and rationally and to avoid risks," Kumble says. "For a businessman, that's a prescription for disaster. In building a business, you don't necessarily act logically or rationally and you take risks all the time.

"Change—change in law, society, business—makes this mandatory. You have to stay one step ahead. That means taking risks and that's precisely why change frightens the firms that criticize us. Because they've always thought like lawyers—because they've always avoided risk like the plague—change scares the hell out of them. Finley, Kumble scares the hell out of them."

5

From the Inside Out: Behind the Client Curtain

"When I heard that Carbide's chairman Warren Anderson was placed under house arrest in Bhopal, I thought, 'Holy Christ, I hope Stichnoth didn't advise him to go there.' "

A legal executive with IBM

On December 3, 1984, Union Carbide's now infamous pesticide plant in Bhopal, India, spewed lethal methyl isocyanate into the air, bringing a wave of devastation that left thousands dead and blinded, and others fighting for life in makeshift hospital wards. The worst industrial disaster in history, the incident assured Bhopal a dark place in history and tarnished the safety record of America's 35th largest industrial corporation, making it an immediate target for multinational ambulance chasers in Europe, the U.S., and India. Within weeks of the disaster —the body count still rising in open-air morgues—20 suits were filed against Carbide.*

The disaster and the flurry of legal activity that followed brought near pandemonium to Carbide's sprawling suburban headquarters adjacent to Route 84 in Danbury, Connecticut, in a bucolic setting that appears, under ordinary circumstances, more like a college campus

---

*The number of suits against the company ultimately reached 120.

69

than a corporate facility. The tranquility was shattered by a flying squad of reporters pressing for interviews with anyone—from harried PR managers to the CEO—willing to venture an opinion (on or off the record) on why the leak occurred, what Carbide would do for the victims, how the corporation would treat its sister plant in Institute, West Virginia, and, most ominously, whether the company would survive massive legal actions. With estimates of the aggregate legal claims rising to $1 billion, Wall Street showed its concern for Carbide's future by selling off shares at a near-panic rate. In two weeks, the corporation's stock plummeted from $48 to $34.

Overnight, as Carbide's focus turned from the marketplace to the courts, responsibility for the corporation's fate shifted from the CEO's office to the general counsel's. As Carbide's head lawyer, 62-year-old John Stichnoth—a polished, soft-spoken gentleman with corn-silk hair and boyish pug nose—found himself in the eye of the storm. His mandate: to marshal the corporation's legal resources to meet the immediate challenge of mounting law suits and to plan a strategy for protecting Carbide's interests in the courts.

But paradoxically, Stichnoth found himself atop a sprawling and expensive legal apparatus incapable of defending Carbide against the Bhopal claims. Like other corporations that have shifted the bulk of their legal work in-house, Carbide has drawn the line at litigation, leaving that to the law firms.

"The corporations recognize that when their asses are on the line—when they're before a judge or a jury that can inflict punishing terms—they need the caliber of attorney they can't attract or retain in-house," says a partner with Chicago's Sidley & Austin. "So no matter how determined they are to be legally self-sufficient, they make an exception when it comes to litigation. Nine times out of ten, when they're faced with a crisis, they look outside, not within, for a lawyer. With so much at stake, it's not the time to nickel-and-dime. Top management insists on the best litigator the corporate budget can buy."

With the potential of a colossal litigation budget supporting Carbide's Bhopal defense, the megafirms, tuned in as they are to marketing opportunities, quickly descended on Carbide and plugged for the business.

"We were literally inundated with offers to help us with the India matter," Stichnoth says, peering through mounds of paperwork looming like snowcaps across his desk. "All made carbon copies of the same pitch. They positioned themselves as experts in mass litigation and, as a sweetener, claimed to have inside connections with the Indian government.

"You'd be surprised to learn how many law firms have personal relationships with the Gandhi family."

Typical of the suitors was the world's largest law firm, Baker & McKenzie. Because it is strong internationally and because it had previously served Carbide in Spain, France, and Norway, B & M's newly elected chairman Robert Cox believed his firm had a good shot at landing at least some of the Bhopal litigation.

"We've opened lines of communication to Union Carbide," Cox whispered soon after hatching his marketing blitz, as if the idea of approaching the Danbury giant was proprietary with Baker & McKenzie. "We're really the ideal firm for them. Our guy in India is expert in this type of matter and has excellent relations with some of the most powerful people in the country. I'd say we've got an inside track on this one."

But it was not to be. Baker & McKenzie's campaign to land a piece of the Bhopal action was doomed from the start. Unlike the national press corps that swarmed around the Connecticut headquarters and left with a headline story, the law firms that descended on Carbide's management* went away empty-handed. In truth, none were seriously considered.

Just why this is so reflects both the increasing complexity of the legal marketplace and the pivotal role corporate counsel play in it. In reviewing the practices and policies of Carbide's Stichnoth and three other influential in-house lawyers (General Foods' Peter DeLuca, Xerox's Robert Banks, IBM's Dan Evangelista), a picture emerges of a diverse market dominated by an eclectic collage of legal executives vested with the power to hire and fire outside law firms. Giant firm partners responsible for building bridges to these corporate lawyers find themselves facing a confusing patchwork of philosophies, biases, and deeply held convictions regarding client–law firm relationships. In Stichnoth's case, they find both obstacles and opportunities.

In a pattern common throughout Fortune 500 land, Carbide's legal department has evolved into a fairly self-sufficient operation that han-

---

*In person and by telephone.

dles 95 percent of the corporation's nonlitigation legal work. Stich-noth's 111-lawyer department is divided into three major practice groups —patents, general commercial, and specialties such as tax, labor, credit, and real estate—and is deeply involved in all of Carbide's far-flung business activities.

Litigation, the gaping hole in the law department's self-sufficiency* and the target market for rainmakers with designs on Carbide's legal budget, is farmed out to a nationwide network of 300 firms, most of which have long-standing relationships with the Danbury giant. The Carbide system—which clearly favors the old-line firms accustomed to institutional relationships—designates lead firms in each jurisdiction, demands that they remain loyal to Carbide, and promises Carbide's loyalty in return.

To remain among the chosen, Carbide's law firms must respond immediately to the corporation's needs—allocating sufficient resources to breaking matters regardless of the staff's involvement with other clients—and must steer clear of conflicting engagements that might prevent the firm from servicing Carbide on short notice. Should Carbide find its Cleveland plant involved in an employee suit, local law firm Squire, Sanders & Dempsey would be obliged to act quickly on its client's behalf even if it were inundated with existing work.

"I'll want assurance that a key partner will be responsible for the work and that he'll be supported by strong number two and three people," Stichnoth says. "It's a rare case indeed when I don't get that assurance. Our law firms want our business and they know that performance and performance alone will keep it. When we call on them, at any time of the day or day of the week, we expect them to be prepared to act on our behalf. No questions, no excuses."

In return for this responsive service, Carbide remains fiercely loyal to its regular firms, giving them first crack at all work regardless of competitive proposals to do it better or cheaper. Aggressive marketers rarely make inroads here: once within the Carbide network, firms are insulated from competitive encroachment unless they fail to maintain Carbide's standards. Because most are high-quality, conservative practices—Gibson, Dunn in Los Angeles, Sidley & Austin in Chicago, Squire, Sanders in Cleveland—this is unlikely.

---

*Only 5 percent of litigation is handled in-house.

That Carbide's commitment to a limited group of firms may deny the corporation the best possible legal counsel in any given city at any given time is of less importance to Stichnoth than the comfort of working with familiar faces that have served the corporation for years. "The devil you know," he says, a coy twinkle in his eye, "is better than the devil you don't know."

"I can read how ABC firm has acquired this fabulous litigator or how XYZ has become preeminent in this or that type of litigation, and I can be impressed by it. But will I change law firms on that basis? Not likely. Just how well a law firm knows the law is only half the equation; the other half is how well it knows the client. I feel strongly about working with firms that know Carbide well—that are familiar with our objectives and our way of doing things. I'm not about to sacrifice that intimacy just because some other firms claim they can perform miracles. They should know better. There are no miracles in the law business."

In a topsy-turvy legal market fraught with mergers and laterals and musical-chair client relationships, Carbide is a stabilizing force. Given high-quality, loyal service, it returns the favor, treating its law firms as true professionals worthy of substantial fees and unswerving fidelity. In a profession now riddled with wholesale fee cutting—primarily as a means of attracting new clients—Carbide refuses to shop the market for lower fees or to shift from firm to firm in a random search for new ideas or opinions. This high-minded approach, still favored by a shrinking cadre of blue-chip corporations, provides a bedrock of fees for the old-line megafirms who are accustomed to it.

The commitment to its professional firms is deeply ingrained in the Carbide culture. In an even more competitive and cost-conscious market, the annual audit, Carbide remains loyal to a 65-year relationship with its public accounting firm, KMG/Main Hurdman, refusing to entertain lowball bids from competing CPA firms, thus allowing KMG to earn a fair profit in its service to the corporation. This is not a license to steal—Carbide carefully reviews fees and places limitations on them—but rather a conviction (a rare one in today's market) that for professionals to perform as professionals, they must be paid accordingly.

"We're not letting our law firms write their own tickets," Stichnoth says as he gazes out the broad picture windows of his smallish but comfortably furnished office. "But by the same token, we're not basing the entire relationship on the size of the fees. That would be short-sighted. Costs are important, yes, but not as important as results. We don't look for cheap law firms; we look for those that win.

"I'll take performance over efficiency any day. If we're being sued for $5 million, I'm far more interested in getting that claim thrown out—or in settling for a fraction of the amount—than I am in reducing the legal fee from $150,000 to $125,000. Good law firms get good results. They earn their fees. That's why we work with proven performers, and that's why we'll continue to do so."

With this philosophy central to his management of Carbide's legal affairs, it should come as no surprise that Stichnoth played deaf to the legal salesmen who came calling in search of Bhopal fees, turning instead to the corporation's long-time regular counsel, Kelley, Drye & Warren of New York.

Once an all-encompassing lawyer-client relationship—with name partner John Drye serving both as a director of Carbide and its general counsel—the arrangement, reflecting the sweeping changes in the legal profession, has diminished somewhat in scale if not intensity. As Carbide strengthened its in-house department and the general counsel became independent of the law firm, Kelley, Drye lost some of its influence over the corporation's legal affairs, especially its access to top management through Drye's position on the board.

But Carbide's legal system—an eclectic mix of the old and new schools—has enabled Kelley, Drye to retain a key role in litigation, getting first crack at corporation's major cases for as long as it meets the Carbide loyalty test.

"The other firms that sought to represent us in the Bhopal litigation were of the strange idea that personal injury litigation was new to us and that we'd be helpless to defend ourselves without their assistance," Stichnoth says. "How preposterous. Kelley, Drye is quite experienced in mass tort litigation, having defended this corporation and other clients in similar actions over the years. What's more, they have the advantage of knowing more about our products and our principles than any other law firm. They were the logical choice to do the work."

Responsibility for the Bhopal suits fell to Bud Holman, former Kelley, Drye managing partner (1966–73) and now lead partner for Carbide. A highly regarded litigator who joined the firm in 1958, he has seen sweeping changes in the profession during his nearly 30 years with Kelley, Drye.

As Holman puts it, "There was a time when large law firms like ours had a partner on the board and could comfortably assume—in recognition of that special relationship—that most of the work would come their way. But that's a thing of the past. Strong relationships are still important, yes, but they don't carry any guarantees. Today clients hire Bud Holman only when they think Bud Holman will do the best work.

"I recognized how drastically things had changed when I was asked several years ago to represent a major corporation in a sex discrimination case. It came as a surprise to me because the client was known to have a close relationship with another law firm. As it turned out, the regular firm was weak in this type of work and so a legal consultant—hired by the client—suggested that I be brought in to fill the gap. That's when they called and asked me to take the job.

"Think about it. I'd never even met one of those consultants and they were giving out my name. That used to be unheard of. Until recently, referrals were based on established relationships, where the parties recommending lawyers were thoroughly familiar with their work. Now it's all a matter of hearsay, word of mouth, that kind of thing. Look, I don't mean to say I wasn't delighted with the recommendation, but it brought into focus just how much this profession has changed."

Although Holman and Stichnoth go to great pains to emphasize that Carbide, not Kelley, Drye calls the shots in this lawyer-client relationship, one wonders if there's not more of the old-fashioned, knee-jerk arrangement here than either party cares to admit. When Carbide's officers and directors were sued by stockholders for allegedly failing to disclose information about defects in the Bhopal plant's safety system, they sought another law firm to represent them. Having Kelley, Drye counsel both the officers and the corporation could be viewed as involving a conflict of interest that management wanted to avoid. A handful of firms—including Sidley & Austin, Sullivan & Cromwell, and Cravath, Swaine & Moore—interviewed for the job, but when the appointment was made, Carbide wound up choosing New York's Cahill Gordon & Reindel, the one firm recommended by Kelley, Drye. While there is nothing inappropriate here, the specter of a lead law firm playing the pivotal role in shaping its client's legal relationships smacks of the old partner-on-the-board approach.

Interpreting Carbide's legal policies can be tricky business. As the megafirms have all discovered, the Danbury giant sends out confusing messages. One one hand, it champions loyal, enduring relationships, leaving the more aggressive legal marketers with little hope of picking off new business through cold calls, seminars, brochures, or the like. Even so promising an opportunity as the replacement of a Carbide stalwart (an occurrence as rare as a total eclipse of the sun) with a competing firm is more of a family affair than an open competition. Such was the case when Carbide replaced its former Chicago counsel Kirkland & Ellis in the late seventies.

"The trouble began when Carbide asked Kirkland for help with what was really just a routine matter and Kirkland responded that it would like to help but was already representing another party in the litigation," says an attorney familiar with the incident. "Because the other firm was a bigger client, Kirkland asked to be relieved of its obligation to Carbide. Naturally, Stichnoth agreed to this—no one wants to work with a law firm whose heart isn't in it—and set out to find a replacement, not just for the case at hand but for all of Carbide's Chicago business. As it turned out, his choice was based on an old friendship, that with Sidley & Austin's managing partner Blair White. They'd been classmates at the University of Iowa and had stayed in touch over the years. Though Stichnoth had always itched to hire White, he'd been hamstrung by Carbide's ties to Kirkland & Ellis. Because both are Chicago firms, it had to be one or the other. The break with Kirkland gave Stichnoth the opening he needed to hire his old friend. What appeared to be a client conflict was actually an opportunity in disguise."

Asked about White, a dewy-eyed Stichnoth can't resist strolling down memory lane.

"Whenever the dean of the law school was asked about Blair, he'd say he had the highest grades of any student; whenever the dean was asked about me, he'd say I had the highest grades. It was a running joke between Blair and me in our college days and we still reminisce about it whenever we get together.

"Clearly, our careers took different paths, but I always kept abreast of Blair's pursuits and was naturally impressed with his accomplishments over the years. Not only in rising to the top of so prominent a law firm as Sidley & Austin but equally in the caliber of cases he has handled. When the American Bar Association prepared its position on legal advertising, Blair represented them. I said to myself, 'If he's good enough to represent the ABA, and, in effect, the legal community, he's good enough to represent us.' "

If ever a law firm was appointed on the basis of an old school tie this was it. But there is a danger in assuming that Stichnoth's penchant for enduring relationships makes him an easy mark for anyone with a history of service to Union Carbide. Yes, incumbent firms and old college buddies hold an advantage they may not enjoy elsewhere, but to remain in service to Carbide, both must perform at high levels. Bud Holman and Blair White, for example, are widely respected as superb practitioners—intelligent, hard-working attorneys who get results for their clients. Were that not the case, neither would remain on Carbide's payroll.

Although Stichnoth can allow himself to be influenced by his outside firms—as in the appointment of Cahill Gordon—he is in no way subservient to them. Nor is he blinded by their mystique. While Carbide's stable boasts some of the most prominent names in the profession, its doors are not closed to less illustrious firms. That the antithesis of mystique, Finley, Kumble, doesn't work for Carbide doesn't preclude that possibility. In fact, Stichnoth semiendorses Steve Kumble's "secret code" that clients hire lawyers, not law firms. At Carbide, both get the nod. Kelley, Drye lands the India work because Kelley, Drye, the firm, generally gets the big Carbide cases. On the other hand, Stichnoth moved his Washington antitrust business from megafirm Jones, Day, Reavis & Pogue's D.C. office when star partner Don Baker, who had serviced Carbide, lateraled sideways to Sutherland, Asbill & Brennan.

"There are two different types of corporate/lawyer relationships," says Baker, who served as Assistant Attorney General in the antitrust division during the Ford Administration. "One that is comprehensive, covering many transactions, handled by many lawyers in a firm, over many years. Carbide and Kelley, Drye fall into that category.

"Then there's the barrister relationship, where the client believes that one specific lawyer is right for one type of case and is more interested in hiring that guy than in hiring a given law firm. That pretty much sums up my relationship with Union Carbide. When I moved to Sutherland, they sort of moved along with me.

"Let me add, however, that this kind of continuing relationship isn't guaranteed. You have to perform for the client and equally important, you have to align yourself with quality law firms—those that wear a badge of respectability. Without that, the client, no matter how much it respects your abilities, may not be able to justify hiring you.''

Asked if Finley, Kumble wears the ''badge,'' Stichnoth answers in a way that would warm Steve Kumble's heart.

''If they had a lawyer with a skill I needed, I'd consider hiring them. There are times when you are looking for an individual, not a firm.''

Carbide's drive for virtual self-sufficiency (minus litigation) in the conduct of its legal affairs forces it to recruit a full complement of talented in-house attorneys skilled in the broad spectrum of legal services once offered exclusively by the outside firms.

This voracious appetite for top talent puts the corporation in direct competition with the firms, not only for seasoned practitioners but even more for the bright law school grads who can be shaped into good lawyers. It is here that Stichnoth the general counsel—Stichnoth the corporate manager—clashes with the law firms as he does on no other matter. The issue is economics.

If the general counsel (of any company) is no longer subservient to the law firms, he is still answerable to the CEO, whose concern is with legal department's budget as well as its performance. To justify its existence, as well as its continued expansion, the law department must demonstrate that it can perform the company's legal duties more efficiently and economically than the outside practitioners. The general counsel's prestige, his position in the corporate hierarchy, hinges to a great extent on his ability to control costs and to prove, ultimately, that he can save the corporation money in the delivery of legal services and in the resolution of legal issues. For both, he must attract capable professionals within reasonable salary guidelines. It is here that the law firms pose a formidable obstacle. By bidding lavishly for the top graduates from the likes of Harvard, Yale, Columbia, Stanford—and by offering starting compensation in excess of $60,000—the firms escalate wage scales, effectively undermining the general counsel's efforts at budget control.

''For a law firm whose partners average $375,000 a year, to start associates at $48,000 or more may be generous but entirely within reason,'' says a senior faculty member at New York University, whose law school is nudging into the elite corps once limited to the Ivy League. ''But not so for a legal department where the corporate counsel earns $175,000 and his senior subordinates top out at $125,000. Starting associates in the $50,000 range distorts the pay scale and inflates the corporate overhead.

"But do the students care about this? Of course not. They're interested in dollars, not excuses. If the Union Carbides of the world want to compete for their services, they'll have to find some way to pay the going rate."

Just the kind of talk that turns the normally unflappable Mr. Stichnoth into a nerve ending.

"That the law firms think they can corner the market on the best students by continuously raising salaries reveals a dearth of business sense. Upping the ante every year doesn't give you a clear advantage; it only forces the competition to meet your price. In the end, everyone loses—everyone except the students who take home those big paychecks. Paying these ridiculously high starting salaries is stupid, insane, irresponsible, and if that's not enough, totally self-defeating.

"If Union Carbide drastically lowered its prices in an attempt to corner the market in any or all of our products, would we be successful? Of course not. Inevitably, competitors would match our discounts dollar for dollar. When the dust cleared we'd all wind up with the same market share but with lower margins to show for our efforts.

"I'll tell you what else really tees me off about those outrageous law firms' salaries. Ultimately, the corporations have to foot the bill. Whatever sum the firms pay their associates, they pass off, with a markup, thank you, to their clients. That's a luxury we don't enjoy."

Traditionally, the big firms have prospered on the spread between associates' salaries and the higher hourly rates billed to clients. To maximize this source of profit, the highly "leveraged" firms surround partners with from three to four associates, each of whom is viewed as a separate profit center. Because associates don't share in the firm's earnings, the income earned on their labors is grist for the partnership draws. The higher the associate-partner ratio, the more profitable the firm.

While leveraging is still a key component of law firm economics, it is increasingly difficult to achieve. As the corporate legal departments have flexed their muscles, they have taken in-house much of the grunt work formerly handled by teams of law firm associates. Why pay a premium for this work, the Stichnoths have asked, when it could be performed equally well (some say "better" because of the insider's familiarity with the corporation) by staff attorneys?

"When we go outside it's to tap a narrow specialty that's needed only occasionally in our business and is therefore uneconomical to staff for on a full-time basis," says the corporate counsel for a Fortune 500 food giant. "And in those cases, we're looking for brains, not bodies. We want a lawyer who knows how to do something very well and who comes without a lot of excess baggage that only duplicates the resources we have internally.

"Those law firms looking to throw hordes of associates at us are living in some kind of twilight zone. Why should we pay them to train people for doing the kind of work we can do ourselves? Because that's the way it used to be done? That's absurd. Just because that nonsense used to be tolerated around here doesn't mean it ever made sense or that it should continue indefinitely. By putting an end to it, I've saved this corporation millions of dollars—probably tens of millions.

"What's right for the law firm isn't always right for the client. Learning that is what it means to 'manage' the legal function."

In railing against the law firm's compensation practices, Stichnoth—and other corporate counsel of similar mind—overlook a key point. The megafirms pay lavish starting salaries not only to lure the top grads but also to perpetuate the myth of superiority. In a culture that equates money with quality, those firms offering the most generous compensation are viewed throughout the profession as the best, the most prestigious, the elite. When Stichnoth complains that "there's an oversupply of lawyers and a scarcity of engineers, but the latter don't command salaries that even approach that of the law firm associates," he's missing the point. By overpaying for talent, the megafirms enhance their position at the top of the legal hierarchy. To students and clients alike, the unwritten message is clear: "Anyone who can afford to pay that much must be good. Very good."

The message is not lost on Peter DeLuca, senior vice president and general counsel for the $9 billion–a–year General Foods Corp. Home to such all-American junk foods as Jell-O, Cool Whip, and Kool-Aid, the White Plains, New York–based package goods giant is also host to a controversial experiment in corporate legal services. One that has observers sharply divided on its merits and its ultimate impact on the profession. To proponents it is the next logical step in the evolution of the corporate legal department; to critics it is a silly charade destined for failure.

Aware of the hubbub surrounding his experiment, DeLuca behaves like the obsessed scientist, protective of his invention but acutely aware that it could still blow up in his face. Since the latter part of 1980, he has been working to create what at first blush appears to be a contradiction in terms: a corporate partnership—or put another way, a law firm within the corporate framework.

"Looking from the outside in, our legal department may appear to be cut from the same mold as all the others," DeLuca says as he lights a miniature cigar in the roomy elegance of his executive office just doors away from General Foods chairman Jim Ferguson. "But from the inside out, it's really quite different. For starters, we refer to our organization as a 'law firm' rather than a 'law department.' The distinction is more than semantic. From the way we recruit people to the way we pay them and involve them in management, this is very much a law firm."

A relaxed, even-tempered executive with a creative streak unusual for corporate lawyers, DeLuca has emerged as a leader of the new genus of corporate counsel. A man with a mission, he is determined to reshape the in-house legal practice from a mass of lawyers shoehorned deep in the corporate apparatus into a semiautonomous entity with a clear and identifiable style. In the process, he hopes to give the law department a mystique of its own, enabling it to compete for the best and the brightest law school grads and to achieve an unprecedented level of operating performance.

DeLuca's plan can be traced to his post-New York Law School days as an associate in the corporate acquisitions practice for New York's Cravath, Swaine & Moore, the Lutece of American law firms. With a closeup view of the firm's client relations and its own internal machinations, he made two critical observations that have influenced his career as a corporate counsel.

"I saw from the start that the outside lawyers play a limited and belated—call it 'after the handshake'—role in corporate acquisitions. As a young man eager to be in the thick of it—to be privy to the negotiations that lead to mergers—I felt frustrated by this distant role and I imagined my peers felt the same.

"But I also recognized that for many associates, everything took a backseat to the single-minded drive to become a partner. The Cravath partnership had a magnetic pull the likes of which I'd never seen before or since. People committed their lives to making it. I was impressed by that and by the way the partners' collective interests shaped the firm into a cohesive unit.''

Impressions that stayed with DeLuca long after he traded his personal aspirations for partnership to assume the general counsel's post at PepsiCo, Inc., a Cravath client, where he served for 12 years until moving on to Revlon and ultimately the top legal spot at General Foods. Arriving at GF's sprawling suburban labyrinth in December of 1973, DeLuca found a disoriented legal department divided by petty fiefdoms and personal jealousies. Corporate generalists, then the prima donnas of the staff, worked independently of the specialists—mostly trademark and patent lawyers—whom they viewed as second-class citizens. Staff quality varied across the lot, with third- and fourth-rate lawyers (mostly law firm dropouts and corporate lifers who viewed the department as a safe haven from uncertainties of private practice) working beside competent if unmotivated professionals who were content to do a good job and go home at sundown. All, regardless of their capabilities, deferred respectfully to the outside counsel, Wall Street's Sullivan & Cromwell.

To DeLuca, who by now was shaping strong opinions on how a corporate law practice should function (as a hybrid of the in-house department and the private firm), this was a caricature of all that was wrong with internal law departments. Lacking the prestige and the economic incentives to attract and motivate high-caliber lawyers, the GF department served mostly as a catch basin for law firm rejects and for those unwilling to test their mettle in high-risk, high-reward law firm careers. As such it could not hope to compete with Sullivan & Cromwell for legal performance and, equally important, for management's respect. With little incentive to perform, to hone their skills, to become better practitioners, the in-house lawyers acted exactly as they were treated: as a ragtag collection of professionals performing isolated tasks independent of one another and without high regard for the corporation's underlying interests.

The problem was compounded by General Foods' growth—both internally and through a series of acquisitions—that glued new businesses onto the corporate structure.

"Our operating divisions grew in number and size, and division counsel began to develop almost as distinct groups, with little regard for the corporation as a whole,'' DeLuca recalled in remarks to the New York State Bar Association. ''But I also saw that they had grown in another direction—away from the main stream of the law department. New specialties required a people commitment, such as litigation, labor, and finance and securities. Each division counsel required an assistant division counsel, or two. I sensed when I came on board too much turf-protecting. Division counsel, in some cases, regarded some specialists as second-class citizens. There was even some unconscionable 'going on the record'—lawyers down the hall from each other corresponding by memoranda. I felt that unless we could come up with an organizational concept and a spirit bought into by everyone which united us as a department, we might end up like a governmental structure with branches, assistants, assistant branch chiefs and chiefs. . . .'' (Speech of April 25, 1984.)

Determined to prevent this frightening specter from becoming reality—and at the same time to breathe new purpose into General Foods' disoriented legal practice—DeLuca began (in that same speech) by asking a series of penetrating questions:

- ''How can we break down the artificial barriers of organization and participate in the totality of our law firm?

- ''How can we avoid the narrow focus of our respective skills?

- ''How can we develop the type of flexibility that allows our law department to respond to the changing needs of the client and the opportunities for innovative service while covering the basic client needs?

- ''How can we make broad experiences in many areas of the law, as well as leadership development, available to all attorneys?

- ''How can we structure, or rather destructure ourselves, so that there is more than one career objective—general counsel—available?

- ''How can we attract and retain the very best?''

The more he wrestled with these questions, the more a single solution began to form in his mind. That of an internal partnership. A law firm within a corporation.

Quietly at first, perhaps fearing his ideas would be ridiculed, DeLuca began pitching the concept over lunches and in informal meetings with corporate management. As he saw it, his bold plan to refashion the traditional corporate law department into a quasi-law firm would erase with one master stroke the negatives long associated with in-house lawyers, would inflate staff egos, and would give GF an extraordinary advantage in recruiting high-ranking law students.

"I guess you could say that my plan was one of those 'if you can't beat 'em, join 'em' strategies," DeLuca says, chain-lighting one cigar with the ash of another. "Try as you might to attract the best students into a law department, you'll strike out so often just because it is a department and not a law firm. Many of the top graduates won't even consider your recruitment efforts. It's an impenetrable barrier.

"So I thought, why not create a law firm here? By changing the essence of this practice, from a department to a firm, I was convinced I could attract the very people that once wrote us off and could give those lawyers already on board a new pride in their work."

DeLuca's plan, which by then had become the worst-kept secret in General Foods, was officially unveiled at the law department's annual staff meeting in September of 1980, where it was received enthusiastically by most of the corporation's 55 lawyers. While some of the old hands (who are about as flexible as their counterparts in the outside law firms) may have snickered over the "preposterous idea" of a law firm within a corporation, most recognized that the change could only improve their station and supported the idea, if only in principle. With DeLuca's brainchild still little more than a flimsy proposal, the staff reserved final judgment until a fleshed-out plan could be developed. Just how would the "firm" be structured? Who would be in charge of what? How would personal and group respon-sibilities change? What would happen to salaries and bonuses?

Aware at the outset that his project would succeed only if it had strong staff support, DeLuca appointed a study group to research the issues and to determine if the plan could be implemented equitably. He knew that forcing lawyers into a "firm"—one they chose not to belong to—would make a mockery of the concept. Most would have to feel, much like the Cravath associates, the "magnetic pull of the partnership." The General Foods partnership.

But the study group found that this would happen only if the "firm" was a firm in more than name alone.

"The special committee concluded, first, that the operating philosophy of our law department could be that of a partnership," DeLuca recalls. "It was pointed out, however, that being a partner means sharing in the direction and management of the enterprise, as well as in the rewards. Said another way, the partners needed a 'large piece of the action' in the administration of the department, in addition to the rewards for success. So a mechanism had to be created for that shared responsibility to become a reality. Secondly, it was stated by this committee that the partnership goals had to be the goals of all, so there was no room for protection of roles or turf. Thirdly, partners had to expect that partnership is a long-term relationship, and they had to do what is required to make it work. Next, we had to identify what level in our department constituted 'partner' and what it took to merit that designation, that is, to make partner. Finally, the partnership level had to be a real one and had to have about it the stature and rewards for which associates in the department would want to strive."

Therein lay the rub. How to create a performance-oriented environment in a plodding, seniority-based corporate system. DeLuca's answer was to devise an ingenious plan that harnessed the corporation's strengths and resources while at the same time diminishing its relative weaknesses vis-à-vis the outside law firms. Working in conjunction with the law staff and corporate management, he dreamed up creative solutions for each of the key stumbling blocks that threatened to knock his plan out of the box before it saw the light of day.

To meet the most critical challenge—how to simulate the law firms' associate-to-partner career path within a corporate setting—DeLuca turned GF's highly stratified pay system (which, in its standard use, resembles that of the bureaucracies he was trying to avoid) into an incentive-driven ladder culminating in financial rewards roughly equivalent to those of a law firm partner.

It works this way: Law school grads enter the corporation at General Foods salary grade 12, a middle management level paying $34,500 a year. With passage of the bar exam, the young lawyer gets his first incentive kicker, rising to grade level 15 and an annual salary of about $38,000. Now he's been officially inducted into the professional staff and his career progress is determined, much like a law firm associate's, in part by merit and in part by seniority. Given satisfactory performance, he moves gradually up the pay scales, reaching senior attorney (level 20 at $50,000 salary) in four years and then the partnership eligibility rank (level 22 at $60,000) in six years.*

"At this point the lawyer knows that he or she is up for partner," DeLuca explains. "This doesn't mean that they're in, only that they're designated partnership material and have two years to prove their mettle to the firm. This is the partnership trial period. Those who come up short by the second year are so informed and are asked to seek employment elsewhere. But those who succeed are immediately promoted to grade level 24, which in our firm is limited to partners."

Reaching this first level in GF's partnership ranks (the equivalent of a private firm's nonequity partner), the newest member of the firm is granted the highest annual increase allowed under GF's compensation policy (18 percent) and gains a voice in the "firm's" management. Two years or so later, the salaried partner gains the ultimate reward, inclusion in the equity ranks (grade level 26), with full participation in General Foods' profit-sharing plan. Like the other GF executives at this senior, middle management level, the new partner is eligible for an annual bonus, based on corporate performance, of up to 30 percent of salary.

Bringing someone into the partnership ranks is more than the kind of meaningless ego boosting that transforms $40,000-a-year bank loan officers into $50,000-a-year vice presidents. With each of General Foods' operating departments limited to a prescribed number of grade level 26 spots—only 19 are allowed for the law department's 75 attorneys—the designation is not made idly. Naming one candidate as a partner means another cannot qualify. Those who do qualify get to share in the corporate profits.

But partnership in DeLuca's "firm" is not limited to financial rewards. To simulate the shared power in a law firm, each GF partner has a voice in how the department is run. The governing body, the Law Department Management Committee, is composed of three permanent members—the general counsel and the two associate general counsel—and four other partners elected from the ranks for two-year staggered terms. Every partner is eligible to run for office and to vote for committee members.

---

*1985 figures

Surprisingly, the "firm" functions much as DeLuca had intended, as a power within a power. Although corporate management ultimately determines the law department's budget and appropriates the funds to meet its expenses, it adopts an arm's-length approach from there, allowing the general counsel and his management committee to run GF's legal affairs with little intervention from above. Just how the budget is spent, how cases are handled, how attorneys are hired and promoted, is decided by the management committee, which takes a decidedly democratic approach to the firm's internal affairs.

Consider the procedure for making new partners—a revealing indicator of a law firm's management philosophy. For a staff lawyer to become a candidate, he must first be recommended by an existing partner, who submits the nominee's name to either of the associate general counsels. Acting as a committee, the partner, the associate general counsels, and the general counsel debate the candidate's qualifications, voting the nomination up or down. The names of those candidates passing this initial hurdle are then placed before the management committee, which makes the ultimate decision. Although a majority vote is required, all decisions—as in most private law firms—are made by consensus. Designed to preserve collegiality, this emphasis on a unanimous decision means that DeLuca's vote is occasionally overruled.

The process is fairer, more thorough, and certainly more intimate than that at many private law firms. Certainly, the partners at GF are more familiar with the candidates for partnership than those at Finley, Kumble or any of the other large, multicity practice firms.

From all appearances, DeLuca has done the impossible. Waving his magic wand, he has created a law "firm" within the bowels of a publicly owned, multinational corporation. Or has he?

"I just took my youngest daughter on a tour of Universal Studios' movie lot, and something there reminded me of DeLuca's little experiment," says a megafirm partner. "You know those houses, saloons, sheriff's offices they've built on the sets. They're just facades. One-dimensional props designed to look like the Little House on the Prairie. Peek around the back and you see it's just an illusion.

"The same goes for General Foods' so-called law firm. It's not a law firm. It's a corporate law department masquerading as a law firm.

"The fact is you can't turn a group of corporate employees into a law firm just by calling them one. That's like calling a lion a fly just because you want to swat it away. Problem is, it won't work. Neither will General Foods' little game of pretend. Anyone who's smart enough to graduate from law school is too smart to swallow the nonsense that he's joining a law firm when all the evidence says law department. He can tell a fake sheriff's office when he sees one.''

The point here—shared by other lawyers familiar with GF's experiment—is that in spite of the trappings of a law firm, DeLuca's department is subject to the rules and policies of the corporation it serves, making it very much a non-firm firm.

''The distinguishing factor between a law firm and a law department is that the former is an independent entity and the latter is not,'' says a partner with Minneapolis-based Dorsey & Whitney. ''The law department exists at the corporation's discretion. Should General Foods chairman decide tomorrow morning that he no longer wants an in-house law department, poof, that department's history. Goodbye, farewell, sayonara. Well, that just can't happen here. No single external force determines the fate of this firm or of its partners.

''Look, one of my old college buddies is now general counsel for a big oil company. Although I haven't seen the guy for years, I noticed in an SEC filing that as an officer of the company he's earning $410,000 a year, has a load of stock options, and a generous profit-sharing plan. At first I thought, 'Christ, what the heck am I knocking myself out for worrying about clients, about controlling our expenses, about growing and surviving as a law firm when this guy just shows up and does better than I do?'

''But then I realized that at any moment that guy's CEO could stroll into his office and on a whim, a bad mood, a burning desire to hire his brother-in-law for the job, whatever, could can him. It happens. And when it does, the guy's on the streets looking for a job. That, thank God, can't happen to me and that's another difference between a law firm and a law department.''

He has a point. Much as DeLuca strides through the eerily silent corridors of GF's new eyesore of a world headquarters (staff lawyers call it ''the Taj Mahal'') as if he were managing partner of a prominent Wall Street firm, he refers repeatedly to senior management's support of the law department. Support that would be unnecessary in an independent firm. And while he claims to have virtual carte blanche in running his shop, there are limitations. Consider this conversation with the author:

Mark Stevens: You say the Law Department Management Committee makes all decisions on running the department. Are these decisions subject to approval by corporate management?

DeLuca: Absolutely not.

Stevens: They have no say in these matters.

DeLuca: Not a word.

Stevens: On none of the issues?

DeLuca: None.

Stevens: What about the size of the department's budget?

DeLuca: Oh, well, on that yes . . . (*Pause.*)

Stevens: And what about the number of profit-sharing partners you want to make?

DeLuca: Well, yes, on that too.

Stevens: Is it accurate then to call yourself a law firm when you're not free to make these key decisions? Like how much money you'll spend and how many partners you'll make.

DeLuca: We all have to live with compromises. For us, that means recognizing that while we can't be a law firm per se, we can function as close as possible to one given the restraints of corporate organization.

One leaves DeLuca's domain with the impression that this is very much a make-believe law firm. That the talk of partners and clients and management committees is a carefully contrived fantasy that becomes real only to those who, like avid theater goers, submit to the "willing suspension of disbelief." They believe because they want to believe.

In spite of DeLuca's claim that the creation of an in-house "law firm" has bolstered GF's recruiting efforts, it cannot even begin to compete with the prestigious megafirms for top students. What success GF has achieved may, in fact, be attributed to its focus on the second- and third-tier schools, leaving the Ivys to the Shearmans, the Skaddens, and the Sidleys of the world. The company's 1984 recruits were drawn from Howard University, George Washington, Georgetown, and the University of Vermont. Good but light years away from Columbia, Yale, and Harvard.

Still, it may be too easy to poke fun at DeLuca's "firm." Perhaps more important than what it is not is what it is and what it has accomplished.

"In order for a law department to break its reliance on outside counsel, it must attract and retain high-caliber specialists in-house," says the deputy general counsel for a Connecticut-based industrial corporation. "This tends to be a real stumbling block in the traditional setup because specialists have no identifiable career path. There's only one general counsel's post and they're not likely to be promoted to it.

"To the extent that DeLuca's system responds to this program by allowing the specialists to aspire to partnership much as they would in an outside law firm, it answers one of the biggest challenges in law department management. With a full complement of skilled specialists in-house, the corporation can handle an ever wider scope of legal matters internally. The need for outside firms diminishes."

From all objective standpoints, GF's "partnership" is a unique and creative concept that manages to fulfill the true potential of the corporate legal department, giving it a pride and a status that is essential to morale and productivity. With partner compensation topping off in the $100,000 range, GF will never attract Harvard Law Reviewers. But it does garner 50 applicants for every job opening, and who's to say that talented Georgetown grads aren't every bit as capable as their Harvard counterparts?

DeLuca's gift is in his understanding of human behavior. As a general counsel, his role is more that of a manager than a lawyer. By giving his people a voice in their own destiny and by cutting them in on the corporate pie, he has melded a diverse group of lawyers into a cohesive unit devoid of the turf protecting that was commonplace before his arrival. What's more, he has made the internal "firm" feel equal to the outside lawyers, not just by raising salaries but by ending the subservient relationship with onetime lead counsel Sullivan & Cromwell and by taking much of the critical legal work it handled in-house. This is crucial. Unless the staff attorneys believe they are the front line of legal expertise, unless they are treated as managers of the law firms rather than as their marionettes, they cannot surmount the inferiority complex that continues to plague many corporate law departments.

DeLuca's accomplishment is significant. Talking independence and achieving it are two different animals. While the folks at American Can—DeLuca's corporate neighbor just across the state line in nearby Greenwich, Connecticut—cite the familiar hard line about the supremacy of the law department vis-à-vis its outside attorneys, the arrangement doesn't appear to support this. In Can's three major legal-intensive activities—corporate acquisitions, financings, and litigation—virtually all the critical work is farmed out to regular counsel Dewey, Ballantine, Bushby, Palmer & Wood, whose star partner, Joe Califano, sits on American Can's board. Countering the widespread move to shift ever greater responsibility in-house, Can's legal spending is still heavily tilted outside, with $8 million of its $12 million legal budget going to law firms and a full half of the outside part, or $4 million, paid to Dewey, Ballantine.

"We have chosen not to supplant reliance on outside counsel with a major buildup of inside staff," says Deputy General Counsel William Ellis, whose drab, cubbyhole office in Can's campus-like headquarters has all the trappings of a corporate Siberia. "In certain areas, which account for much of our legal work, we believe the law firms are better equipped, in terms of readily available talent, to serve our needs."

One gets the distinct impression in some law departments that management is in awe of the outside firms and considers the partners' skills superior to those of the in-house staff. If this is communicated (even subliminally) to the law department, it can only foster feelings of inferiority. Giving the law firm top billing automatically reduces the staff lawyers to second-class citizenry.

With his mix of experience on both sides of the client curtain—first at Cravath and then in-house at PepsiCo, Revlon, and GF—DeLuca is acutely aware of this. Although he refuses to say anything negative about his Cravath days—holding only that they are "a superior firm"—if his experience was typical there were jokes aplenty about the corporate clods on the other side of the legal fence. Much as they bubble over with compliments for the new breed of corporate counsel, law firm partners are convinced of their higher calling and, especially in firms that boast long-standing client relationships, of their indispensability.

Once on the client side, DeLuca was quick to dispel Sullivan & Cromwell of any such notion.

"When DeLuca took over, an antitrust matter came in that under his predecessors would have automatically gone to Sullivan & Cromwell, not because they were the best at it but because they automatically got most of the work that came in here," says a GF insider familiar with the episode. "But DeLuca knocked their suspenders off by turning instead to Kaye, Scholer.* Why? Because they have a hell of an antitrust practice, that's why. It seems only natural but it actually marked the beginning of a new era at General Foods. One in which law firms were picked for their skills."

In first choosing Kaye, Scholer—which remains his favorite outside law firm—DeLuca was moving toward a more flexible arrangement where the law firm acts as a business adviser as well as a legal gun. (Skadden, Arps, also a GF law firm, pioneered this dual role.)

"I can ask the Kaye, Scholer partners their opinion on a proposed settlement," DeLuca says, "and they'll say—minus the ands, ifs, or buts—if I should try to do better or if I'll wind up blowing the deal I already have. Because these are real judgment calls, law firms are often reluctant to take a position. But I can ask Kaye, Scholer real-world questions and get real-world answers."

This much said, DeLuca has been careful not to trade one incestuous relationship (Sullivan & Cromwell) for another (Kaye, Scholer). His in-house "firm" handles the great bulk of GF's legal affairs, including corporate acquisitions, financing, and labor litigation. The outside work is farmed out to a stable of about 30 firms headed by four heavyweights: Kaye, Scholer; Mudge, Rose; Gibson, Dunn; and Skadden, Arps.

All of the firms serving General Foods are managed by DeLuca's law department, which clearly retains the upper hand. GF's Policies and Procedures for Retained Counsel, the bible by which outside firms must live, makes this abundantly clear:

---

*Kaye, Scholer, Fierman, Hays & Handler, a New York firm.

- "... it is to be recognized that the General Counsel of General Foods Corporation has the primary and ultimate responsibility for the legal affairs of the corporation. ..."

To dispel any notion that the law firm has carte blanche in setting hourly fees, in assigning personnel, or in billing the client for its services, the bible sets the following conditions:

- "An estimate of the overall expense of litigation or other matters handled, and the duration of the required service, shall be made as early in the assignment as possible and shall be periodically updated. In the case of litigation, this should be communicated to the Litigation Manager. As to other services, the communication should be with the Department counsel who initiated the assignment, unless otherwise directed by the law department.

- "Prior to any suit, the hourly charges (or manner of determination and estimates, if hourly charges are not to be utilized) of counsel assigned to a specific piece of litigation shall be agreed upon. If circumstances necessitate any change thereafter, it should be discussed with the Litigation Manager. As to services other than litigation, the fee schedule should be discussed with the Law Department counsel who initiated the assignment."

To further insure that legal bills do not run away from their original estimates—a problem as common among law firms as defense contractors—the bible further stipulates that

- "The receipt, on a monthly basis, of a statement for services and costs is preferred by the department. In any event, however, a statement should be rendered no later than ten (10) days following the end of each calendar quarter in which services are rendered. The statement shall include a tabulation of the professional time expended, as well as description of the nature of the service rendered. When appropriate, particularly in protracted complex litigation, the person who rendered such service should also be identified."

The last two provisions are designed to stop the law firms from bill padding, a practice that was all too common before the DeLucas of the world began demanding detailed invoices.

"When clients allowed—I guess I shouldn't use the past tense because some still do—what I call a bottom-line invoice, we could bury everything in that bill including the managing partner's golf club dues," says a former megafirm attorney now active in investment banking. "The bottom-line bill gave the total fee, broken down perhaps in three or four subdivisions with scarce detail on how the client's money was spent.

"When the numbers were big—say anything over $250,000—we could bill for associates who were essentially filling space until they passed the bar, we could tack on 25 percent or more to hourly fees, and we could bill two clients for a lawyer's total hours even though he worked for each only half the time.

"I even know of a firm—thank God we never went that far—that would figure how much they wanted to make on a case and then work backward from there, structuring a bill to arrive at the target amount.

"That always reminded me of a guy I knew who owned a telephone answering business. Because he knew his busy customers, mostly doctors, dentists, and lawyers, didn't keep records of all their calling activity, he'd routinely tack on 15 percent to their monthly bills. If an internist's charges came out to $300, for example, he'd make it $345 and would send a bill for the total amount without breaking down the charges. His customers' lax controls protected his little scheme.

"But when a client, like General Foods, demands a detailed breakdown of its legal bills replete with names and responsibilities, the fun and games are over."

DeLuca's law firm–law department—call it what you will—has taken the challenge of controlling the corporation's legal affairs a step beyond the Stichnoth approach, balancing the outside law firms' power with an internal equivalent of near-equal stature, while still leaving the Kaye, Scholers and the Skadden, Arpses with a clear place in the scheme of things. But for Bob Banks, vice president and counsel for Stamford, Connecticut-based Xerox Corp., this doesn't go far enough. An outspoken, often bitter critic of the law firms, he turns to them only grudgingly and then with the disdain the firms once reserved for their corporate clients.

Appointed Xerox general counsel in January 1976, capping an eight-year career in the office equipment maker's law department (preceded by a six-year stint with DuPont), the silver-haired, nattily tailored executive has pursued a management policy influenced, at least in part, by the injustices suffered at the hands of the law firms he now hires and fires.

"When I first started with this corporation, there was an unwritten rule that the inside lawyers had to check virtually all of their major decisions with the outside lawyers. This practice wasn't unique to Xerox. It was standard operating procedure at most law departments. You'd come up with a decision on a particular matter and the senior attorney or the general counsel would say, 'Run it by the law firm.'

"Damn if that didn't rub me the wrong way. I'd think to myself, 'Why the hell do I need someone outside to check my work? Am I incompetent? A fool? A trainee?'

"But then I recognized that it had nothing to do with me. Instead, general counsel were so conditioned to accept the prevailing view that they were inferior to the outside law firms that they couldn't make an important decision without the firm's approval. Tell someone that they're bad or ugly or stupid long enough and they believe it.

"Well, if there's a sure way to discourage superior legal talent from working for corporate law departments, it's to treat them this way. So when I became general counsel, one of my first moves was to put an immediate end to the double checking. From that day on, when Xerox's law department made a decision, that was the decision we lived by."

Banks, whose sneeze of an office in Xerox's world headquarters is about the size of the private restroom in a megafirm managing partner's suite, acted to cut costs as well as to restore flagging egos. "The checking system was utopia for the law firms. Every time a decision was reviewed, a bill was rendered. This played right into their hands. The Xerox lawyers would do all the hard legal work and the law firms would get paid handsomely for checking it. What a racket! There was so much waste around here you could cut it with a knife."

Much of the waste was attributable to the law department's rampant insecurity. Since its inception in 1967, it had grown in tandem with outside legal services instead of replacing them. With the requisite checking and double checking of staff work, the department was unable to act without the advice and consent of the corporation's two principal law firms, Wall Street's Simpson Thacher & Bartlett, and the Rochester, New York,* firm of Harris, Beach, Wilcox, Rubin and Levey. Given this redundancy, the law department—designed initially to cut costs—actually increased legal spending.

"The standard gag around here held that the best way to triple legal fees is to start a law department," Banks recalls.

But the general counsel did not see the humor. Determined to reverse the corporation's spiraling legal costs, Banks acted swiftly to end the law department's self-imposed paralysis, bringing virtually all legal work in-house. Relations with Simpson Thacher, which had begun to cool during his predecessor's tenure, were further strained as attention shifted from the law firm to the care and feeding of the internal staff.

Dividing the law department into functional specialties, Banks built up in-house capabilities in SEC practice, antitrust, labor relations, and real estate. Limiting the law firms almost exclusively to litigation, Banks buzz-sawed their fees from a 1977 high of about $15 million to about $3 million in 1984—peanuts for a $9 billion–a–year multinational giant. Adding in the expense for Xerox's 75-lawyer internal staff, legal fees have still halved since the bulk of the work was shifted in-house.

Proud as he is of the savings—in part because of its impact on Xerox's bottom line and in part because he loves to stick it to the law firms—Banks insists that the move in-house would have proved beneficial even if added to the corporation's legal bills.

"We're providing better legal service than the law firms are capable of," Banks asserts, stabbing a finger in the air as if he were poking an invisible megafirm partner in the chest. "Not because they don't have talented and intelligent people. Certainly they do. But so do we, and our people know more about this corporation than outsiders could ever hope to learn."

With this claim, Banks reverses the standard order of superiority, placing the staff attorneys above their law firm brethren in skills as well as costs. A claim that enables corporate counsel to justify their departments on more than economic grounds.

"It was in the midst of a major antitrust suit in the 1950s when we recognized that to give this corporation the best possible advice,

---

*Xerox's former headquarters city.

legal counsel had to be part of the company, not outside of it,'' recalls IBM general counsel Dan Evangelista. ''That recognition gave birth to our law department. We saw that the ability to anticipate problems and to stay on top of them once they emerge is best done by inside lawyers. That's why most of our work is handled in-house. Litigation—the only major exception—generally goes to Cravath, Swaine & Moore.

''Although Cravath is a fine firm, they couldn't duplicate, from the outside, the caliber of work our law department does on the full range of IBM's legal affairs. That's because we require our lawyers to do what can never be expected of outside counsel. That is, to stay fully abreast of this corporation's business activities before they become public knowledge. That means attending meetings, reading documents, staying up to speed on everything going on here.

''If our lawyers first learn of a new IBM product once it's come out of R&D and been released to the press, we've failed. Because if that product—its design or pricing—violates a consent agreement, it was our job to know about it before it hits the market. After that, it could be too late. We protect against that by making our lawyers part of the fabric of the corporation.''

To achieve this at Xerox, Banks has created an intensive training program that requires all new grads hired by the corporation to rotate through four subdisciplines of the law department. In typical fashion, a young woman fresh out of N.Y.U. would serve her first year or two in environmental practice, moving on to stints in the international, antitrust, and SEC practices. After completing the eighth and final year of formal training, the lawyer is assigned to a permanent position either as a staff specialist or as a line counsel to Xerox's operating managers. She is also elevated to an inner circle within the law department—one similar in appearance, if not substance, to that at General Foods.

''The eighth year represents a benchmark in the lawyer's career, signaling his rise to an equivalent of partnership,'' Banks says. ''At this point, he's eligible for 'full attorney' status, meaning he can commit the law department to a legal decision without first gaining approval from a staff superior. It's our way of saying, 'You've arrived.' ''

Banks, DeLuca, Stichnoth, Evangelista & Co. claim that the staff lawyer's knowledge of the business and his increasing stature within it make him every bit as capable as the outsiders and ultimately more valuable to the corporation. But there's another side to the story—one that proud and perhaps resentful general counsel would be loath to admit. That is the undeniable fact that most of the truly remarkable attorneys are real partners in real law firms. While the big corporations are busy conjuring up any number of ego-flattering illusions to attract and retain competent lawyers, the real stars are and will remain on the more lucrative side of the client–law firm relationship. Those with the skills to command a half-million dollars or more a year as law firm partners will not accept $100,000 as a staff attorney whether he's called "senior attorney," "full partner," or "Chief Justice."

A fact that is hardly lost on corporate management. While the CEO will buy the claim of equality for routine legal matters, when the corporation's back is up against the wall, he'll reach for the most prominent names money can buy.

Xerox is no exception. When the copier giant found itself knee deep in a major suit with SCM, which charged Xerox with monopolistic practices, Banks turned to a prominent antitruster, Kaye, Scholer partner Stanley Robinson. By the same token, when it comes to politically sensitive assignments in the nation's capital, Xerox says thanks but no thanks to its law department, referring the matter to D.C. superstar Bob Strauss, a name partner in Dallas-based Akin, Gump, Strauss, Hauer & Feld.

Close examination of Banks's strategies—and those of like-minded general counsel—confirm that while the rise of the modern law department has shrunk the market for law firms, it has created a corridor of opportunity for those firms savvy enough to seize it. By projecting an aura of invincibility in key practice areas—such as antitrust and M&A, where corporate clients feel most vulnerable—and by making themselves home to a stable of superstars, the business-minded firms assure their survival in spite of those general counsel who may prefer to see them on their knees.

The fact is that the new independence of general counsel has put a greater premium on superior lawyering. Without this prized quality, law firms will struggle, often unsuccessfully, for survival. With it, they will be virtually immune to the pressures that will sink lesser competitors.

Undoubtedly, the Bob Bankses of the world will continue to chip away at the law firms' markets, at their fees, at the once-privileged position from which they drew their power. How effectively they fight back depends on how indispensable their service is deemed to be.

"I don't tolerate any nonsense with fees," Banks exclaims, waving a letter in the air. "This law firm, whose name shall remain anonymous, informs me that they're raising their fees. Want to know my response? To hell with that. That's my response. Why allow a 10 percent increase when inflation's only 4 percent? That kind of bullshit isn't tolerated around here anymore and they should know it.

"How will I handle this? Very simple. My secretary will type a very brief letter this afternoon telling the dear lawyers that no, their fees to Xerox aren't going up by 10 percent. They'll then have two choices: to agree with me or to become Xerox former lawyers. Somehow I think they'll see things my way.

"This kind of unwarranted increase isn't the only thing that ticks me off. The hourly billing system itself is chock full of disincentives to lower legal costs. Because law firms make more money the more hours they bill, they have every reason in the world to pile on the hours. That's why I'm exploring an entirely new billing system with our Los Angeles firm Latham & Watkins, whereby the law firm has a vested interest in being cost-conscious and where we both gain if they are. Under this approach, we'll sit down with the firm to determine just how much it will cost to handle a certain litigation. That becomes the working budget the firm is expected to live by. If they go over, we share the costs under a certain formula. On the other hand, if they come in under budget, we split the balance that was budgeted but not spent. The firm gets less money than was originally budgeted but more than it cost them to handle the case. We're looking for a case to test this on. It will be good for the law firms and good for us."

Perhaps, but this trial balloon would likely burst in midair were it floated at Skadden, Arps, considered indispensable to a good many corporate M&A strategies. Asked about Banks's innovative fee proposal, a partner with a major New York–based firm responded this way:

"Imagine this scenario. A natural resources giant has enormous mineral reserves that at current market prices far exceed its book value. But Wall Street is slow to catch on and the stock languishes. Sensing opportunity, Carl Ichan goes after the company, buying up millions of shares and threatening a takeover. Top management sends an SOS to Skadden's Joe Flom, requesting his services on an emergency basis. The world's premier takeover lawyer is inundated with work but finds a way to squeeze in the new client. As he strides into the boardroom, he's met by an appreciative CEO who sits him at the head of the table. As everyone knows, control of the corporation is at stake.

"Just as Flom is about to speak, the general counsel darts in asking him to agree to budget the case and return half the fee if he winds up spending less. Everyone is shocked. But not for long. Within seconds, the general counsel is muzzled and led away. As soon as he's disposed of, the board signs over a blank check, payable to Skadden, Arps. Rules, they say, are meant to be broken. Ditto for legal budgets."

6

Making Money, Making Rain

"When I left my old law firm to become general counsel here, I had one compelling priority: To make certain my former colleagues didn't charge this client what I used to charge it."

Legal V.P. for a bank holding company

Peter Mullen, executive partner of Skadden, Arps, Slate, Meagher & Flom, peers out at the corporate towers that loom beyond the big picture windows of his near-airborne office as if they were giant salt and pepper shakers ready to spice the sandwiches he occasionally gobbles down at his long and orderly desk. A 58-year-old corporate attorney, with Skadden, Arps for more than a quarter century, Mullen epitomizes the brazen self-confidence that some see as Skadden's unofficial trademark.

In the years since its founding in 1948 as a minuscule partnership between Messrs. Skadden, Arps, and Slate,* the firm has risen like a sphinx, shaking up the legal profession, rewriting the rules for success and in the process displacing the venerable institutions that considered their place atop the legal hierarchy to be a divine right.

---

*The three had practiced previously with the predecessor to Dewey, Ballantine, Bushby, Palmer & Wood.

As titular head of the firm that everyone knows is dominated by chairman and name partner Joe Flom,* Mullen wears three hats: strategic planner, chief operating officer, and semiofficial mouthpiece. A shrewd attorney and a crafty media manipulator, he carries off the multifaceted assignment with considerable aplomb. And he appears to relish every minute of it—especially the opportunity it affords him to tout Skadden's success to those now envious competitors that looked down on it as recently as a decade ago.

Considering Skadden, Arps's extraordinary success, it is easy to forget that the firm spent its first 15 years as a relatively unknown corporate and litigation practice competing with a hundred other firms in the midranks of New York's legal community. Only when Flom, then a senior corporate lawyer, began making a name for himself as a brilliant tactician in the corporate proxy battles of the 1960s did major clients start beating a path to Skadden's door. This led to a virtual stampede as Flom's skills in the proxy wars were transposed in the midseventies to the volcanic merger and acquisition market, then primed for a violent eruption that has continued. As hostile takeovers grew rampant in corporate America, chief executive after chief executive scrambled for Flom's services. An early architect of M&A strategies, he became known as a superman in a lawyer's pinstripes.

"Whenever I see that Kentucky Fried Chicken commercial that says, 'We do only one thing, chicken, and we do it right,' I think of Joe Flom," says an associate general counsel for a major east coast corporation. "He devoted himself, body and soul, to developing the merger and acquisition practice before it was all that significant a source of fees and while it was still considered slightly better than ambulance chasing by the big law firms then focused on banking, finance, and the traditional corporate practices.

"But when the merger thing broke wide open—when corporations started PacManning each other like a school of starved piranhas—he emerged as the father of this new practice—this new legal art form. Suddenly everyone, I mean everyone, wanted Flom on their side, and they wanted him at whatever price he asked. Why? Because he did one thing, mergers and acquisitions, and he did it right."

With his reputation firmly established, the demand for Flom's time

---

*As one Shearman & Sterling partner puts it, "Peter manages the firm but Joe owns it."

far exceeded his ability to service it. Credit Flom and his partners for seeing this not just as a source of pride for the firm, but instead as the nucleus of a megapractice. Rather than allow the client demand he could not handle personally to drain off to competitors, the master effectively cloned himself, training a cadre of disciples and sending them out in the field to practice M&A the Joe Flom way. If the star himself was unavailable, clients were comforted by the knowledge that others, under Flom's watchful eye (as Skadden would never fail to assure them), were on the case. This, in a nutshell, was the birth of a major law firm.

M&A proved to be the ideal foundation for a highly prosperous law firm. Because Skadden filled a market void with its unique legal skills and because it served clients in some of their most sensitive and critical transactions—where billions of dollars or perhaps the corporation's very survival was at stake—fees could soar beyond the standard charges for more traditional corporate services available from dozens of prominent firms.

"When a patient learns he'll need open-heart surgery, he doesn't start haggling with the doctor over the fee," says a partner with New York's Parker Chapin Flattau & Klimpl, stretching his face across his desk as if to dot an exclamation point. "Hell no, he wants the best damn cardiologist who ever took the Hippocratic oath and the heck with what he charges. The guy's life is hanging in the balance.

"Similar story with merger-acquisition-takeover practice. To the corporate world, this is life-and-death stuff. The client wants to get its hands on an acquisition it is certain will propel earnings, will add to its industry stature, and will make folk heroes of top management. Or, when the tables are turned, that same client is seeking protection from other carnivores that want to mount its head above the corporate mantel. In either case, the stakes are breathtaking, the deadlines impossible, and to be successful as the hunter or the hunted, the law firm has to throw a talented and experienced staff into the fray within hours. Because Skadden, Arps can do it—and because the business community believes it can do it better than anyone else—it commands incredible fees."

"There's a real paradox in Skadden's M&A relationships," says a partner with Chicago-based megafirm Baker & McKenzie. "The same general counsels that now yodel about their independence and about how they review a thousand candidates before they hire a law firm for any particular case think M&A–Skadden, Arps, M&A–Skadden, Arps, M&A–Skadden, Arps. The way I look at it, they're back to reliance on a single firm even if it's for only one facet of their legal needs.

"To further the paradox, though Skadden played a role in breaking up some of the old, exclusive legal relationships—it was the first boutique firm many clients turned to in breaking with their lead counsel—Skadden has now adopted one of the characteristics of those relationships. Just like the exclusive firms used to charge pretty much whatever they saw fit, because there was no competition for the business, Skadden too writes its own ticket. Its reputation is so awesome that it has the closest thing I know of in this profession to a blank check."

Skadden, Arps's great coup is in its leveraging of an entire firm on the prominence and reputation of a single man—Joe Flom—who may well be the greatest rainmaker in the history of the legal profession. In merchandising its takeover guru, the firm has created an enormously profitable retainer program that capitalizes on the merger frenzy and rewards Skadden for its greatest asset, Mr. Flom himself. More than 250 clients pay annual retainers of from $40,000 to $200,000—in some cases just an insurance policy making it certain that the miracle worker and his squadron of highly trained shock troops will be available at the first sign of a takeover.*

Figuring a conservative $50,000 per client, the retainers generate roughly $12.5 million in annual fees. Because some of this booty is never soaked up by lawyer time—remember, some clients are paying simply to have Flom & Company's equivalent of the Strategic Air Command on round-the-clock alert—these are high-margin revenues.

Lest this sound like a license to steal, Skadden's chief administrative officer, Earl Yaffa—a refugee from Big Eight accounting firm Arthur Young—volunteers that clients can cash in their unused M&A chips for other Skadden services.

"We still believe in making money the old-fashioned way—by earning it," Yaffa jokes, mimicking the familiar John Houseman–Smith Barney commercials. "Clients who pay M&A retainers but don't use us for that work are encouraged to apply the money to litigation,

---

*Most, however, pay the retainer as part of a wider legal relationship that extends beyond M&A work.

communications, financings—any other type of legal representation we offer. We're here to service clients, not to take their money."

Fair enough, but Yaffa—who, as a layman surrounded by attorneys he's supposed to manage, appears at times like a lion tamer hoping like hell the big cats will respect his whip—omits two little tidbits that are the whipped cream atop the retainer pie. Yes, M&A fees are legal currency in the Skadden, Arps system, but—and here's where the business-minded firm's marketing prowess comes in—rather than a charitable concession this is an effort to cross-sell the firm's services. Skadden's top priority of the 1980s was to reduce its once-lopsided dependence on M&A—a goal it has accomplished with as much skill as it brought to bear in building that practice. The retainer mechanism has been in perfect sync with this master plan.

The retainer system, Skadden, Arps style, is ingenious: it draws in clients through the M&A practice, assures the firm of a healthy fee base, and encourages further use of (and dependence on) Skadden through the redirection of retainer dollars to other practice units. Whether clients make use of this trade-in program is of minor consequence; in either case, Skadden gains.

Because clients are often tight-lipped about their relationship with Skadden, Arps (much of which is attributable to the secrecy and related paranoia that surrounds mergers and acquisitions), it is often difficult to determine who pays how much for what.

Asked if American Can, a Skadden, Arps client, barters its unused M&A retainer dollars for other legal services, Can's deputy general counsel Bill Ellis appears surprised at the question—as if it was the first he'd heard of the exchange offer—and then delivers a fudgy response that raises more questions than it answers.

STEVENS: Do you make other use of the Skadden, Arps M&A retainers that aren't used for M&A?

ELLIS: They have given us some sound advice on mergers and acquisitions.

STEVENS: But if you don't use all of your retainer in this way, do you make it up on other services?

ELLIS: They have strengths beyond M&A. Peter Mullen, for example, is an excellent corporate lawyer.

STEVENS: Do you use him for that?

ELLIS: Well, I don't want to characterize the extent of our relationship with Skadden, Arps.

STEVENS: You've talked freely about your relationship with other law firms. With Dewey, Ballantine. With Covington & Burling. Why not do the same with Skadden, Arps?

ELLIS: Our retainer relationships are a much more sensitive issue. Let's just leave it at that.

American Can is not the only firm that shrouds its Skadden-M&A relationship—or the question of whether one exists at all—in a veil of secrecy. IBM's general counsel Dan Evangelista, an open book on much about Big Blue's legal affairs, goes CIA when the topic turns to Skadden, Arps.

STEVENS: Does IBM have an ongoing relationship with Skadden, Arps?

EVANGELISTA: Not that I can think of.

STEVENS: More specifically, although a takeover of IBM would be quite unlikely, does the corporation have Joe Flom on retainer?

EVANGELISTA: Well, we have spoken to Joe and to Peter Mullen— who we know quite well—from time to time, but I am not aware of a retainer relationship.

STEVENS: If there was one, would you be aware of it?

EVANGELISTA: I imagine so.

STEVENS: But you don't know of one?

EVANGELISTA: I can't say.

STEVENS: Would you be willing to look into it and let me know?

EVANGELISTA: I don't know that we'd want to reveal that either way. I think we'll pass on that.

The aura of indispensability evoked by the M&A practice (terribly difficult for law firms offering traditional services to duplicate) allows for the exceptional fee arrangements Skadden commands. In addition to the retainer system—the envy of all the megafirms—Skadden adds to its considerable wealth by levying a "performance premium" where its work brings the client substantial rewards. Here, the standard time-based fee is doubled or tripled.* In this way Skadden mimics the investment bankers it works closely with on takeover battles, earning, like the deal makers, a transactional rather than an hourly fee. Because this smacks of greed (expected of investment bankers but not of "learned professionals"), Mullen and Yaffa, generally given to unabashed braggadocio concerning Skadden's earning power, refuse to cite specifics on the performance premium.

"I'm not going to reveal any hard and fast rules for charging premiums because there are no such rules," Yaffa waffles. "But I will tell you that billable hours are only part of our fee. We also factor in how well we perform, what kind of pressures we have to work under, and the unique skills we bring to a case. If Joe Flom, Roger Aaron, or another of our partners comes up with a creative strategy that affords the client exceptional results, our bill's not going to be limited to what's on the time sheets."

An in-house counsel with contacts at Skadden offers this uncensored glimpse of the fee-setting procedure:

"From what I gather it's a little art, a little science. The top five or six partners who call the shots on all the heavy-duty merger and acquisition deals sit around with Yaffa and Mullen and decide how valuable they were to the client, and what the client can afford to pay. Their objective is to come in with a number that'll get paid sans any embarrassing objections from the client. While they're not timid about demanding the premium when all else fails, they'd prefer that it be part of the unwritten rules of hiring Skadden, Arps, Slate, Meagher & Flom for takeover work."

No doubt, cutting itself in on the client's gain is the best way for a law firm to step up its earning power. But this is possible only when it can offer what clients believe is a truly unique service.

---

*Mullen says that fees may be reduced below the standard hourly rates when client deals go bust.

"About three years ago, one of the law firms we use tried to charge a premium for some good but very routine work in helping us negotiate the sale of a subsidiary," says the in-house counsel. "Need I say they were eating that invoice for dinner. Not that the quality of their work was at issue. It was just fine. But I knew we could have gotten equally good results from dozens of firms without paying a penny over the hourly rates. No way was I going to pay the premium.

"By the same token, were a strong M&A firm to bill us a premium for defending the company from Saul Steinberg, Christ I'd have to say we'd pay it. Not just because they deserved it but because we'd never know when we'd want to use them again."

Skadden's preeminence in a critical practice specialty, and the mystique that goes with it, boosts its performance in the four key components of law firm profitability:

- Hourly fees: With its attorneys in great demand, the firm can keep its hourly fees at the high end of the spectrum. This translates into $85 per hour for associates fast out of Harvard or Yale, $160 for senior associates, and among the partners $170 for the freshly minted, $225 for the "mere mortals," $300 for the "stars," and $300-plus for Flom (who, virtually all agree, could charge $1,000 an hour and get it).

  "The only limitation on Joe's fees is his own good sense not to be a pig about it," says a partner with Cleveland megafirm Jones, Day, Reavis & Pogue. "The guy's too much of a class act to rape his clients."

- Leverage: With an associate-to-partner ratio of more than three to one, Skadden is at the high end of the leverage curve. Here again, the M&A specialty serves the firm well. While the Peter DeLucas, the John Stichnoths, and the Bob Bankses of the world are actively limiting law firm engagements to partner-level expertise—taking most of the staff work in-house and in the process putting pressure on law firm ratios—M&A is an exception. Because few corporations have significant M&A expertise on staff, when they hire Skadden for takeover work, they hire a team of partners and associates. The practice is immune to corporate penny pinching.

- Utilization: With Skadden's services on everyone's shopping list—thus keeping the staff permanently occupied—partners and associates post high chargeable hours, averaging more than 2,000 a year with some climbing to the stratosphere of 2,500 or more.

■ Realization: Because few choose to quibble with Skadden over fees, a high percentage of these hours are billed and ultimately collected.

With these profitability components reinforcing one another, Skadden turns in impressive numbers, generating fees of $129 million a year (tops among the megafirms) and net operating income of $58.5 million. At more than 45 percent, the firm's estimated profit margin—a key yardstick of a well-run firm—bests such prominent megafirms as Weil, Gotshal by more than 10 percentage points.* Partnership shares are also among the highest in the profession, topping out at more than $1 million for the stars, including, of course, the Guiding Light.

The atmosphere at Skadden's midtown New York headquarters at 919 Third Avenue is coolly modern, evidencing success and money minus the predictable portraits in oils and heavy-handed mahoganies favored by the Shearmans and the Milbanks. Here, the interior design is minimalist, with sleek, lacquered furnishings allowing the Manhattan skyline to speak for itself. The mood is optimistic, confident, ambitious, and firmly rooted in the present.

By thinking and acting like businessmen as well as attorneys, Flom & Company have pulled the rug out from under Wall Street's sleeping giants, forcing them, at an ungodly age, to play catch-up ball. Fearful of missing the boat on highly profitable M&A business and, perish the thought, of allowing their long-time clients to slip away, inexorably, to Skadden and the other aggressive players among the giant law firms, such white-shoe stalwarts as Sullivan & Cromwell, Simpson Thacher & Bartlett, and Davis Polk & Wardwell have been making noises in M&A, but only as distant runners-up to Skadden.

Whatever their position on the M&A hierarchy, the mere fact that once-indomitable legal practices are now modeling themselves after "the firm that Joe built" speaks more to Skadden's success than its bulging coffers do. Time and again, senior partners admitted, always

---

*Figures from the AM LAW 50, *American Lawyer*, July/August 1985, pp. 4, 5, 11.

in hushed tones befitting an exchange of nuclear intelligence, that they viewed Skadden as the firm to emulate.

"As lawyers, they're not a whit better than us," whispered a megafirm managing partner who asked the maitre d' at his favorite New York luncheon bistro to trade his usual prime table for one barely removed from the kitchen (and the welcome clatter of dishes) the day he agreed to go deep throat on Skadden, Arps. "In fact, I'd vouch that their standards for partnership are lower than ours. One of the fellows they just made partner had been around the horn with the headhunters a few years ago. We looked at him and were not at all impressed. Not as an associate, much less as a partner. Don't ask me to point to anything specific. There was just a consensus here that the fellow lacked something as a lawyer and, maybe this scared us more than anything, that he'd try to walk on his colleagues' bones the day his name went on the letterhead—if it ever did. You can't have that in a team culture like ours.

"But from an organizational perspective, Skadden, Arps has created something a lot of us who don't think we have anything to learn can learn from. They've worked it out so that the system—including lateral hiring, new practice offices, and partner compensation—reflects client and marketing considerations rather than the firm's internal politics. Shit, I've been struggling with these issues for five and a half years now with no progress at all.

"The difference is a recognition from the top down that you have to be market-oriented. That you have to behave like businessmen and apologize to no one for it. But when I've suggested at executive committee meetings that we borrow a page or two from the Skadden firm, I've been shot down by some of my closest friends. They suggested that if I was so enamored of Mullen's ways that I should go out and ask him for a job. While I have no intention of doing that, I'm not about to stop prodding the firm I love to shape itself more like the ones I think will eat us all alive unless we do."

Skadden partners love this kind of grudging reverence. The institutional arrogance that permeates the firm is evidenced by their supreme confidence and at the same time the tendency of some partners to deride and belittle more traditional firms as hobbled relics of the Mesozoic era. As classic switch hitters, they preface their verbal attacks with the charitable refrain that they'll never criticize another law firm and then, without missing a beat, segue into their verbal assaults. Consider these random opinions:

- On Los Angeles stalwarts Gibson, Dunn and O'Melveny & Myers: "They must be doing something wrong because a month after we opened our Los Angeles office, we were taking M&A business away from them.* True, we're well known in that practice, but LA's their home field and you'd think they'd have put up a better fight than that."

- On Shearman & Sterling:
  "Years ago, Citibank didn't blow its nose without calling on Shearman & Sterling. Now they're starting to show real independence. Some of the work is being spread around to other firms, and now that Reed is in the driver's seat, that trend—which can only benefit the bank and us—will accelerate.

  "As for Shearman, I'm not terribly impressed with their ability to adjust."

- On Paul, Weiss:** "A firm trying desperately to get with it, to loosen up its act, but with little success. With everyone there worried what Judge Rifkind† will think and everyone afraid to cross him, no one makes decisions. The place is paralyzed."

- On Cravath, Swaine & Moore, the only major New York firm with a reputation, and some say partner earnings, superior to Skadden's:
  "They're about 10 years away from a rude awakening. By pretending to be above the 'crude' marketing tactics the rest of us have had to adopt, and by holding themselves somehow superior for it, they're playing with a time bomb. One with a long fuse, I'll admit, but a time bomb just the same. Sooner or later the market will catch up with them. They'll have to change. By then, they may find themselves minus a big client or two.

---

*Sources familiar with the Los Angeles market confirm this, agreeing that Skadden scored quickly with its bicoastal takeover practice.

**New York firm Paul, Weiss, Rifkind, Wharton & Garrison.

†Name partner and firm patriarch Simon Rifkind.

"Until now, Cravath's been protected from Mother Nature by a unique group of clients that have allowed them to resist change. But the image they're cultivating—I love the PR photos they plant in the newspapers showing the partners all sitting around the conference room smoking pipes—is out of whack with what most clients expect from modern law firms. Sooner or later, theirs will feel the same way."

■ On Dewey, Ballantine: "Good example of a firm that fell behind the times and is now struggling to come back."

■ On Donovan, Leisure, which, after losing lead client Eastman Kodak, went into a nosedive that saw the departure of many highly regarded partners: "A classic case of doing just about everything wrong. They were too dependent on one type of practice and, worse than that, were living 25 years behind the times."

To be fair, Skadden has not cornered the market on mud slinging. A nasty side effect of the cutthroat competition in accounting, law, and the other once-gentlemanly professions that have fallen victim to it is the willingness of apparently civilized men to savage each other in private conversation. When the slings and arrows are leveled at Skadden, Arps, partners at its giant law firm competitors enjoy downgrading the firm's proudest asset, M&A skill, by claiming that it places a poor second to that of its smaller rival, New York's 90-lawyer Wachtell, Lipton, Rosen & Katz. To Peter Mullen, that charge is like having a sharp butcher knife twisted in his spinal cord. Confronted with the charge, the normally even-tempered partner struggles to control his emotions. Literally fuming, he mumbles almost incoherently about an *American Lawyer* piece* that he believes created this perception, adding that it royally pissed off Skadden's litigators, who took monumental umbrage with the magazine's assertions.

Whatever the cause of the perception, the "second place to Wachtell, Lipton" charge is a sensitive issue, in part because it may be true ("Flom created the takeover practice," says a Jones, Day partner,

---

*The *American Lawyer* of March 1984 (p. 42) quoted an attorney who had worked with Skadden and Wachtell as saying, "Wachtell is like the old Yankees with Joe DiMaggio, Mickey Mantle, Whitey Ford and Yogi Berra, while Skadden is like the Chicago Cubs with Ernie Banks. They don't have any good litigators."

"Marty Lipton, father of the poison pill, made it an art") and in part because as a fast-track firm on a 20-year roll, Skadden is hardly accustomed to criticism (except from dog-tired associates in the M&A department who call the place a "sweatshop"). But as the firm solidifies its position atop the legal hierarchy, it will find that the attacks it levels behind closed doors will boomerang increasingly in its direction. Success breeds imitation, yes, but it also breeds jealousy, contempt, and a concerted effort to knock the leader on its butt.

If the unflattering comparison to Wachtell, Lipton riles the Skadden boys, another more serious criticism haunts management, including Flom, Mullen, and the vanguard of younger partners poised to assume leadership of the firm. It is that Skadden, as one of its partners said Donovan, Leisure had become before its nosedive, is still too dependent on "one type of practice."

Ever since Flom's name became synonymous with M&A and Skadden, Arps grew in tandem with that reputation, critics have questioned the firm's ability to sustain itself on the strength of a specialty highly vulnerable to changes in Wall Street's fashion cycles. When mergers and acquisitions retreated from their record pace, they asked what would happen to the law firm that built a huge infrastructure on this shaky practice.

Credit Skadden's high command for asking the same questions and for acting early on to cultivate additional practices. Although Flom is generally credited with designing the diversification program that has brought Skadden a significant presence in the general corporate, real estate, banking, and bankruptcy practices, Mullen, as one Skadden partner puts it, "made the thing work. He was a driving force in the cross-selling effort that brought M&A clients into other parts of the firm."

Mullen was also instrumental in the hiring of Earl Yaffa, who, as Skadden's managing director, has two distinct roles: chief administrative officer and staff marketing director. In the former capacity, he is concerned primarily with the back-office functions (financial controls and administration) in which law firms have been traditionally weak; in the latter, he orchestrates Skadden's diversification strategy, seeing to it that all elements of the puzzle fit neatly together.

Just how Yaffa came to Skadden reveals the forward thinking that is part and parcel of the firm's approach to the business of law.

"I was a CPA and a partner with management responsibility in Arthur Young's New York consulting practice," Yaffa recalls, "when a group of my people were carving out a specialty in law firm consulting. Because the volume of work in this area was growing and because it had potential written all over it, I decided to get my feet wet by participating in some field work.

"As it happened, my first law firm client was Skadden, Arps, which at the time—in late 1979—had about 200 partners and was struggling with the growth pains that are inevitable when a professional firm experiences extraordinary growth.

"At this point, their administrative functions were just kind of limping along rather than being professionally managed. They needed a lot of help with financial controls, management structure, and administration of the back office. While Peter and others watched over these things—and recognized their importance—the firm had grown so fast and furious that this part-time surveillance was woefully inadequate. To the firm's credit, they recognized this and asked Arthur Young for help in hiring a person to serve as the executive in charge of administration."

As the interviewing began—with Arthur Young and Skadden, Arps principals interviewing prospects (mostly corporate management types strong in EDP)—the profile of ideal candidate quickly changed from that of an administrative closet case that would be relegated to the back room (the kind of glorified bookkeeper law firms typically hired to look after their purses) to a general manager with day-to-day responsibility for all of the firm's business functions.

Skadden changed directions in part because it was disappointed with the stream of applicants it was seeing and in part because it realized it was already staring across the table at the best man for the job. An experienced management generalist with strong computer expertise, Yaffa was ideally suited to give the firm the coat of management varnish it needed to navigate through the next stage of growth. But getting the CPA-consultant to relinquish 17 years of seniority at Young to take on what was by all accounts an experimental position would take some hard sell, including upgrading the position to give Yaffa direct-line reporting to the administrative committee and assuring him a big paycheck (estimated at $300,000).

Eventually, Yaffa succumbed and was anointed a quasi-partner, thus creating a new wrinkle in Skadden's organization. As the only nonlawyer with real decision-making authority, a window office, and a six-figure salary, he was immediately an unequal among equals. The riddle of how to deal with the nonlegal professional manager became both Skadden's and Yaffa's first challenge. Would the partners respect his mandate to enter the senior ranks minus the legal training long considered a prerequisite for this privilege? Would the partners—and worse yet the associates—consider themselves his superior, his boss? Would the boys of the bar take pot shots at the CPA (a species of professional traditionally viewed by lawyers as a lower form of life) in their midst? The answers were of interest beyond the confines of 919 Third Avenue, to all of the megafirms suffering related growing pains and searching (some say "groping") similarly for solutions.

From all accounts, Skadden's experience will lead others to follow suit. Despite some hand wringing on Yaffa's part, petty politics have rarely surfaced. To the contrary, the partners have responded favorably to his skills and initiative in bolstering the business side of the very commercial venture that is Skadden, Arps. Although his rank is clearly a notch below that of full partner (he cannot, for example, share in the firm's earnings in the same way as a partner), he has more power and influence than all but the heaviest hitters in the partnership ranks. Consider this further testimony to the firm's business instincts. That Yaffa can contribute to the bottom line, that he can be instrumental in the drive toward efficiency and practice expansion, is reason enough to respect his operating DMZ.

Perhaps Yaffa's most significant contribution is his ability to relate the firm's still awesome growth into its grand design for broad-based diversification.

"We never just open an office and leave it alone to fend for itself," he says, speaking in the measured tones that are genetic to accountants. "Our concern is to integrate that office into the firm, to open the lines of communication, and to methodically plan its development.

"Consider the Chicago office. From the outset,* its value to us was twofold: as a presence for Skadden, Arps in a key business center and to further develop certain practices—such as real estate and public

---

*The office was established in May 1984, when Skadden recruited five former partners from Chicago's Mayer, Brown & Platt to launch the firm's presence in the windy city. Six associates were hired soon after the office opened; this number has grown to more than 40.

finance—that are important to us nationwide. With this in mind, we have worked the office from both ends, cultivating local clients in Chicago and making that office's expertise available to clients throughout the firm. It's a synergistic process. That's how you build a law firm.''*

For a heterogeneous firm replete with a smorgasbord of lawyers from varying socioeconomic backgrounds, religions, and political affiliations, Skadden is a remarkably cohesive unit. Save for occasional infighting between the M&A princes and their partners in other practices, one detects more harmony here than in other aggressive firms of its size.

Although this can be explained simplistically by the Kumbleism that making money is the greatest glue of all—and there is undoubtedly more than a dollop of truth to that—Skadden differs from other hardheaded business-minded practitioners in that it has recognized the dangers of wholesale mergers and has studiously avoided them. Unlike Finley, Kumble, which is promiscuous in its mating habits, Skadden is highly selective and favors laterals (which have less of an impact on the culture) to mergers. The results speak for themselves: while other firms are strung together with a stack of partnership documents, Skadden's partners work together without a written agreement on firm governance. In spite of this, Skadden has never lost a partner to another law firm.

Impressive? Absolutely. Who can argue that this is not a magnificently managed firm with a sterling reputation and a gifted group of attorneys? But the question still nags: is the firm too dependent on one type of practice? Judged purely by the numbers, the answer, as Mullen is quick to point out, is no. No, no, no. But as many a chief executive has discovered, numbers can be deceptive. Sometimes, what appears on the balance sheet just ain't necessarily so. Same for Skadden statistics. True, M&A fees account for a third or less of the gross. True, the firm can deliver a full complement of legal services. True, more than half the partners work outside of M&A. But . . . but no matter how you crunch the numbers, to the business community that hires

---

*Through this and similar efforts in a broad spectrum of practice disciplines, each geared to a perceived need in the marketplace, Skadden has managed to diversify to the point that M&A represents from 25 percent (Mullen's claim) to 35 or 40 percent (outsiders claim) of aggregate fees.

law firms, pays the retainers, coughs up the premiums, this is the premier M&A law firm in the world and there's just something exciting and sexy about working with the firm that holds that distinction.

"If the client's lawyers aren't impressed, the CEO is," says a consultant to prominent law firms. "They want the bragging rights to having Skadden, Arps or Wachtell, Lipton protecting their interests like a bunch of Doberman pinschers.

"It's a status thing. If you're a someone and you're getting divorced, you hire Louis Nizer. If you're a someone and you need clout in Washington, you call Bob Strauss. And if you're a someone in the boardroom, you tap Skadden or Wachtell. Get clients to see you in that light and you're going to be very substantial investors in tax shelters."

As undoubtedly are many of Skadden's partners, all of whom have profited handsomely from the firm's M&A glitz. But what will happen when this practice declines, as it inevitably will, due to a slowdown in mergers and acquisitions or a government-imposed ban on takeovers—or when Joe Flom, the 63-year-old wellspring of the Skadden mystique, leaves the firm? Certainly, Skadden, Arps will not shrivel up and fade away. It has built too impressive an infrastructure and too capable a backup management team for that. But it is safe to say that it will lose its trump card and the basis on which it draws much of its power, lots of its fees, and most of its prestige.

Thus the danger of building a law firm on the shoulders of a rare and virtually irreplaceable individual. Once clients can no longer be assured that Joe is on the case—or at least available should the call go out for a resident genius—Skadden's special glow will fade like that of an aging star no longer so ravishing in the closeups. The end of an era.

Another street-smart New York firm both blessed and cursed with a towering personality who has become somewhat of a legend in his own time (although not quite of Flom's magnitude), is fellow megafirm Weil, Gotshal & Manges. Housed blocks away from Skadden, Arps in General Motors' muscular edifice facing the Plaza Hotel at the gateway to Central Park, Weil, Gotshal is home to 339 lawyers and one impresario–conductor–marketer–dreamer–visionary–manager–catalyst–antitrust litigator and rainmaker supreme, Ira Millstein. Virtually everyone in the profession has a favorite story about him.

"I'll never forget the time we were sitting around in a conference room, waiting for Ira to show up for a meeting," says an in-house attorney who has seen Millstein in action. "He'd been held up at the airport or some other such thing and, totally out of character for the very punctual Mr. Millstein, he was about 20 minutes late. Those of us already there used the time to reaffirm a course of action we were determined to take and that we wanted Weil, Gotshal to pursue in our interest. That was the way it would be. Open and shut.

"Well, Ira suddenly appears in the midst of this closed-minded setting and in what appears to be one simultaneous action, opens his briefcase, reads the mood of the group, and begins convincing us to take a completely different approach. We're all sitting there with our mouths wide open (I could almost see tonsils wherever I looked) unable to talk because the guy won't give anyone an opening and because what he says is so damned smart no one wants to admit we'd considered any other approach. In an hour, everything we'd planned to do is reversed, Ira dashes off just as he'd come in and we all go back to work. With charm and verve and sheer force of personality, he'd gotten his way. We'd been outsmarted and outclassed and we all knew it. No one better than Ira."

Says another observer of the Millstein method:

"Ira's a smoothie when he wants to be—mostly in the company of clients—but behind closed doors he's as sharp as broken glass. And tough—no one's tougher. That toughness permeates the whole firm. Once, when I was late for a meeting, I called Ira's office to say that I was stuck in traffic. When I explained this to the secretary, she listened dispassionately and snapped, "No excuses. When should I tell him you'll be here?"

Like his contemporary Joe Flom, the 59-year-old Millstein joined his firm when it was still a lilliputian New York practice serving a menagerie of undistinguished, often nickel-diming clients and turned it into a gutsy, gambling legal powerhouse with a national reputation and a full complement of corporate giants paying dearly for its services. Flom used M&A as the linchpin for leveraging Skadden's rise to prominence; Millstein performed similar miracles for Weil, Gotshal, using both his reputation as an antitrust attorney extraordinaire and his marketing prowess to propel the firm to the top.

A David Susskind lookalike who absolutely exudes affluence from the shock of stylishly cropped white hair to the cut of his immaculately tailored four-button wool suit, Millstein, a Columbia Law School grad (class of '49), holds court in a handsomely decorated 32nd-floor office filled with an eclectic mix of law journals, career mementos, and (read into it what you will) a black-and-white photograph of Albert Einstein. Rarely seated—his energy level is so intense one can hardly imagine him buckling into an airplane seat—Millstein paces the room, gesticulating, frowning, laughing, scolding, complaining, boasting, and, one gets the distinct impression, constantly evaluating his performance, what it will net him and when it will be time to go on to something else. Something more productive.

This restless striving coupled with a first-rate legal mind and incurable workaholism brought Millstein to the attention of the Fortune 100 (where he counts many current clients) when he successfully represented Associated Merchandising in a 1962 antitrust action brought by the Federal Trade Commission. Because the case drew national attention, it gave Millstein an instant luster and drew an impressive parade of deep-pocketed clients (led by General Electric) to his door.

With his star rising, he reportedly pressed Weil, Gotshal's management, notably Sylvan Gotshal, to parlay the firm's growing prestige and expanding client roster into a master plan for aggressive growth —a plan that would bring Weil, Gotshal into the ranks of the nation's leading law firms. To implement this, Millstein and fellow up-and-comer Todd Lang demanded key roles in the firm, which was then still a small operation. When Gotshal balked, the young Turks made it clear that they were moving ahead and would not take no for an answer. When the dust cleared, Millstein and Lang had their way and were effectively in control of the firm.

The brasher and more impatient of the duo, Millstein wasted little time in expanding the firm's horizons. In a move that would prove enormously important to the firm's ultimate growth, he lured a young bankruptcy lawyer, Harvey Miller, to Weil, Gotshal after seeing him in action in the 1969 bankruptcy proceedings of the investment firm of Ira Haupt & Co.*

At the time, the move drew scant attention from the major law firms, most of which regarded bankruptcy practice (as they did tender contests and M&A) as food for scavengers. But Millstein, reading the

---

*Millstein had been retained by bankruptcy trustee Charles Seligson, then Miller's employer.

built-in crystal ball that is standard equipment with true visionaries, believed that bankruptcy would emerge as a significant practice. In time, Miller proved him right. The new recruit turned out to be a superb practitioner (as Millstein had noted in the Haupt proceedings), an Olympian rainmaker, and an astute manager who led the bankruptcy practice to the kind of explosive growth that, along with antitrust and litigation, propelled Weil, Gotshal to the ranks of the megafirms.

Today, the ruling clique of Millstein, Miller, and Lang preside over a firm boasting 83 partners and offices in New York, Houston, Miami, and Washington, D.C. In addition to the key practice departments of antitrust (led by Millstein), general corporate (Lang), litigation (Millstein again), and bankruptcy (Miller), the firm is active in tax, securities, banking,* real estate, labor, sports, and entertainment. Major clients include GM, GE, J. C. Penney, Westinghouse, Columbia Pictures, NCR, and Harper & Row.

The three co-managing partners are said to share power equally. While this may be an accurate reflection of the organization chart, charts are not Millstein's forte and there is little doubt that he is the firm's leader in most critical aspects from rainmaking to creating the blueprint for continued growth and expansion. In interviews with attorneys, bankers, clients, former clients, and academics it is clear that one personality—Millstein's—is the one by which the firm is most closely defined.

"Every time I ask my secretary to write a letter to them, I pause for a moment, certain I've made a mistake," says one attorney. "You know why? Because I keep looking for Millstein in the firm name. Subconsciously, I think it should be Weil, Gotshal, Manges & Millstein."

This overlapping identity between a law firm and one of its partners (again in the manner of Flom and Skadden, Arps) is due in Millstein's case to his consistent ability to identify promising markets and his persistence—in spite of doubting Thomases among his partners—in moving Weil, Gotshal in that direction before the old-line firms awake to the potential. For a modern law firm to escape its humble beginnings and to encroach successfully on the turf once reserved exclusively for

---

*Weil, Gotshal is one of the few firms to make substantial inroads in the Shearman & Sterling–Citibank relationship, having picked up healthy chunks of business in bankruptcy and consumer banking.

the white shoes, a dominating, earth-shaking personality is indispensable.

"I don't think that Weil, Gotshal is any better or any worse from a technical standpoint than the other 20 largest firms in the country," says Stuart Freedman, vice president–law for the big insurance brokerage firm of Fred S. James & Co. "But they use a Millstein innovation that distinguishes them from the competition. I think of it as an 'account executive approach.' Rather than fighting the move toward in-house practice and the streamlining of fees and services, they make an attempt to work with the client to accomplish these objectives. The way I understand it, they meet with clients, discussing budgets and fees, and spelling out how they will approach the case. By taking the offense in the law firm–client tug of war, by indicating that they want to work with you rather than just for you, they're seen as modern, flexible, responsive. Millstein deserves the credit for that. He was smart enough to recognize client concerns when they were still in the embryonic stages and to go out and to address them in a meaningful way. He's very smart."*

Millstein is the pluperfect example of the new breed of megafirm managing partner. Forever moving ahead, snubbing his nose at traditions, challenging the status quo, he pushes relentlessly for multicity expansion, incentive-based compensation, the cultivation of boutique practices, and the exploration of new markets. His sponsorship of the firm's Washington, D.C.–based telecommunications practice provides a revealing glimpse at the Millstein modus.

"I was a hot commodity," says former FCC Commissioner and telecommunications expert Joseph Fogarty, referring to his status in the Washington legal community in June of 1983, when he was preparing to leave the Commission after a seven-year term. "Because I'd specialized in telecommunications issues—because I was the only Commissioner at the time to do so—I was being actively recruited by virtually every law firm in the country that wanted to practice, or was already active, in the burgeoning telecommunications market. West Coast firms, New York firms, midwest firms—they were all at my

---

*Not every general counsel is impressed with the account executive approach. Offers to help budget his department's work prompt Xerox's Bob Banks to "reach into my back pocket and take a firm grip of my wallet."

door. And I'm not talking about headhunters. The managing partners were doing the knocking.''

A retiring, button-down type whose manners are more like the bureaucrat he was for 20 years* than the high-octane Weil, Gotshal partner he is now supposed to be, Fogarty found himself in position to more than quadruple his $68,000 government salary and to win instant partnership in one of the major law firms—all of which hoped to parlay his FCC experience into long-distance fees from telephone company clients. With the ball in his court, Fogarty insisted that the successful suitor accept a package deal: the Commissioner would come complete with his secretary and two former FCC staff attorneys.

''Although some of the firms balked at this, a number agreed to my terms and it was up to me to choose among them,'' Fogarty recalls. ''It wasn't easy. Because this was a critical point in my career, I wanted to make the right choice. So I met with them all several times. I asked questions. I asked friends and associates for their opinions. I got all the facts I could need to make an intelligent choice. But when it came down to the nitty gritty, I had to go on the basis of personal chemistry. That is, who impressed me most and who I believed offered me the best opportunity for success.

''On that, there was really no contest. Ira Millstein just stood out from all the others. The man impressed me enormously. He was smart—smart as hell—and he had an enthusiasm for the new practice that, quite frankly, I found contagious.''

Without a significant telecommunications practice of its own, Fogarty's turnkey operation (the Commissioner and his mini FCC staff) matched Weil, Gotshal's needs to a T. With a single stroke, the firm would have expertise, connections, clout in the telecommunications market. To Millstein, as good a tactical marketer as there is at Procter & Gamble, this was the ideal foundation for what would become a substantial telephone practice and, equally important, was a superb way to play catch-up ball in a practice area the firm had been slow to develop.

One tempting piece of business—the kind that law firms must have had in mind when they competed for Fogarty's services—was soon dangled before the former Commissioner's eyes. Telephone executives

---

*Fogarty served as counsel to the Senate Commerce Committee before being appointed to the FCC by President Ford in 1976.

from United Telephone and Continental Telephone called with word of a trade association being formed by the major carriers and an invitation to Fogarty to represent it.

Naturally, Fogarty wasted no time in pursuing the offer. Soon after leaving the FCC, he boarded a plane—accompanied (no surprise) by Ira Millstein—for Kansas City, home of United Telephone, to meet with the executives and others involved in forming the Exchange Carriers Standards Association, a group then being formed to replace AT&T as the standards-setting body for the industry (a role Ma Bell could no longer legally play after divestiture).

To the lawyers' delight, it became obvious from the start that there was no question that Fogarty (read "Weil, Gotshal") was being asked to represent the organization—that was a given—only about the extent of the services his firm would provide.

Millstein smelled opportunity. As an emerging organization in the sensitive and highly litigious arena of telecommunications, the ECSA would need general corporate, antitrust, and tax counsel as well as Fogarty's expertise. As his newest partner watched in awe, Millstein spun a web of marketing synergy that showcased Weil, Gotshal's range of services and that set the stage to capture business for many of its practice departments.

"I saw then and there what it means to think like a businessman and a lawyer," Fogarty says. "After all those years with the government, that was clearly something I had to learn. And I did. Working with Ira and Todd, seeing how the firm pulled together to achieve common objectives—all of that helped me develop the right approach, the right way of looking at things. I refer to this in-house training as my 'Weil, Gotshal lobotomy.' "

But has the training paid off? Has Weil, Gotshal earned a respectable yield on its telecommunications investment? Yes and no. Although Fogarty has picked up some respectable business—including the ECSA and Continental—none of Weil, Gotshal's existing clients have shifted their telecommunications work from the powerhouse practices (such as Sidley & Austin) to Fogarty's relatively dinky operation. Minus this key element of practice synergy—and the failure to develop really substantial fees from telephone companies—the effort must be considered only a marginal success. But Millstein has not panicked.

"You can never rest on your laurels in this firm," Fogarty says, glancing over his spacious, well-appointed office almost as if he still has to pinch himself to believe he's there. "Weil, Gotshal doesn't accept the status quo. So although I feel we've made progress here— we've gone from two lawyers to six, which I guess is okay growth— I can't say I'm satisfied with that.

"But Ira's told me not to worry. That if I keep doing good work, the business will come. By serving the trade association well, he says, we'll impress the member companies who in turn will hire us for their own needs. He has confidence and so do I."*

Just as Fogarty looks to Millstein for guidance, for direction, for faith, for hope, for inspiration, for a pat on the back, so too does much of the firm—and many of its most important clients—gravitate to the charismatic litigator. In fact, if Weil, Gotshal has a problem, it is that in some circles, Millstein is seen as the firm. Or at least as the most exceptional thing about it.

"Weil, Gotshal is an excellent firm at Ira Millstein's level," says a New York–based lawyer/investment banker. "But once you get past Ira, and maybe a couple of the other senior guys, it can drop off like a ski slope. What I'm saying is that I don't think there's great depth there."

Says Union Carbide's John Stichnoth, "If I hired Weil, Gotshal, I'd want to work with Ira Millstein. He's a superb attorney. That would be my reason for choosing them."

Adds another lawyer, "When I think of Ira I'm reminded of the story of the town in the old west that's suddenly invaded by a gang of outlaws who are getting drunk and rioting on Main Street. The sheriff can't possibly handle the situation and so he telegraphs the Texas Rangers for help. When he goes to the station to meet.the lawmen, he's amazed to find that only one ranger got off the train.

---

*Weil, Gotshal's formula for success—specifically its willingness to wait patiently for new practices to develop—is virtually identical to that espoused by Peter Mullen at an *American Lawyer* seminar. "We have established three general criteria (for success): short-term economics, long-term economics and absorption into the firm. . . . For us, short-term economics is the least important, unless there is some dramatic impact on the firm, and we have not experienced that at all. Long-term economics is a more important consideration and we might very well be willing to wait through several years of marginal economics if we feel that the long-term potential is sufficiently high. . . ." (Quoted in "Going National," *American Lawyer*, December 1984, p. 17.)

Hearing his complaint, the ranger responds, 'There's only one riot, isn't there?' ''

What happens when Weil, Gotshal's ranger is no longer available for rescue missions? Like Skadden, Arps when Joe Flom exits, Weil will not collapse like a house of cards. The infrastructure, the bankruptcy practice, the client momentum are far too substantial for that. But clearly, there will be a black hole where Millstein once sat. What it sweeps up into its magnetic field may be hard to predict, but undoubtedly something very dear will be missing.

From one standpoint, Skadden, Arps may be better prepared for the loss of its spiritual leader. While Flom has consciously stepped away from day-to-day management of the practice, Millstein, along with Lang and Miller, keeps his fist wrapped tightly around the lines of power. And by jealously guarding their control of the firm, the triumvirate may have precipitated one of the most damaging, and embarrassing, setbacks in the firm's recent history: the overnight loss of its real estate practice.

The story begins in 1979, when Millstein played the lead role in landing noted New York real estate rainmaker Charles Goldstein, then a partner with New York's Schulte Roth & Zabel. A legal nomad, typical of the prized laterals who come complete with clients, fees, prestige, and profits, Goldstein had previously performed his impressive services for two other firms. Viewed as "our lawyer" by some of New York's biggest real estate operatives (the status Roy Cohn enjoys with the city's celebrities) and therefore blessed with lucrative legal relationships, Goldstein must have ranked high on dozens of lateral hit lists.

"Guys with big reputations and big clients can literally auction their services to the highest bidders," says William Burggraf, president of Catalyst Legal Resources, a headhunting outfit. "They can ask for a million a year, for limousines and apartments and unlimited expense accounts. In fact, they don't even have to ask for it; if they're that good, others will offer it to them. Law firms, personnel recruiters, and assorted intermediaries will come a'courting whether they've expressed an interest in leaving their current firms or not.

"Everyone, they say, has a price and the pursuers all believe they can structure a package that will hook the star and bring him on board. At least they all try."

Weil, Gotshal succeeded not only in snaring Goldstein but in landing most of the team that had worked with him at Schulte Roth & Zabel. The group—which in effect became Weil, Gotshal's real estate department—thrived in the bigger firm, streaking to more than 40 lawyers and becoming one of New York's premier real estate practices.

Until it departed as suddenly and dramatically as it had come. In January 1985 Goldstein abruptly announced to the Weil, Gotshal high command that he was moving across town to the big, politically connected firm of Shea & Gould, again transporting most of the real estate department with him and virtually decimating Weil, Gotshal's property practice (leaving it with one partner).

The defection had more to do with power than money. From all accounts, Goldstein was earning into the seven figures at Weil, Gotshal, and could have pressed the firm for more had that been his objective. Instead, he was seeking a commodity Millstein himself had fought for earlier in his career: a voice in the management of the firm. That he was unsuccessful—or just thinks he was unsuccessful depending on who you ask—points up the dangers inherent in laterals and their effect on synergy, collegiality, and glue. No one knows this better than a highly interested observer (and likely previous bidder for Goldstein's services), Steve Kumble.

"The perception in the legal community is that Charlie Goldstein—excuse me, he insists that you call him Charles—was never integrated into the Weil, Gotshal practice," Kumble says. "It seems that he was never made part of the firm's overall management. But as I understand it, that will change at Shea & Gould and that's why he's going there."

Interviewed soon after the Goldstein diaspora, Millstein—whose low tolerance for losing is legendary—fusses and fumes, trying desperately to belittle the loss and to shift the blame on Goldstein, repeatedly reminding a visitor that the real estate rainmaker had performed his revolving-door routine at other firms before coming to Weil, Gotshal. Acknowledging that Goldstein's clan had never been fully absorbed into the firm, he attributes this to Goldstein's preference for his own people rather than to the managing partners' refusal to share power.

On the contrary, Millstein holds that for a successful law firm to remain so, the men at the top must relinquish control while they are still healthy and vital, making room for the next generation of talented and ambitious partners. A process he insists has already begun at Weil, Gotshal with the establishment of a management committee.

As to his personal timetable, Millstein claims he will give up his management duties (but not the practice of law) sometime between the age of 60 and 65. Whether he can live up to this pledge is a matter of opinion.

"If Ira says he'll retire from management at a certain date, then that's when he'll do it," says the managing partner with a midsize New York firm. "He's a man who makes a statement and then backs it up."

Another senior partner sees it differently. "Some guys don't retire even after they die. The imprint they've made on the firm is such that they continue to run the place from the grave. Everyone keeps saying, 'What would Ira think, what would Ira think?' In a way, they're as influential when they're not there as when they were. That, I think, will be Ira's legacy."

7

Today Cleveland, Tomorrow the World

"You can't be a malevolent dictator, keeping partners against their will. Try it and they'll protest with their feet."

Howard Trienens, chairman of
megafirm Sidley & Austin

Dick Pogue, Jones, Day's national managing partner and the legal profession's version of a banana republic dictator, learned the hard lessons of national practice over the chilled corpse of his father's career.

The story starts with an axe murder and ends, more than a half century later, with a bloodless coup in the nation's capital.

It was in the jerkwater town of Red Oak, Iowa, that a bright and bookish farm boy, Welch Pogue, witnessed the trial of a sensational homicide that had all of southwestern Iowa buzzing in 1918. Only 17 at the time, Pogue was so taken by the proceedings that he decided— much as budding actors do when they see their first stage play—to pursue a career in law. Driven by his dream and by a determination to break the ancestral force that tied generations of Pogue men to the land, young Welch went off to the University of Nebraska and the University of Michigan Law School and ultimately landed about as far as one can get from the farm (and axe murders) in corporate practice with the starchy Boston firm of Ropes & Gray.

Quickly established on a lucrative career track that offered great promise to a young man with impressive legal skills, Pogue might have served out his years doing bond offerings for Boston-based companies had he not been smitten by an emerging industry—the airline business—which at the time (late 1930s) had all the glamour and excitement Silicon Valley holds for today's generation of up-and-comers. With the fledgling airlines facing a host of virgin legal issues and with the rapidly expanding carriers competing for authorized passenger routes, Pogue saw an opportunity to shape and define a body of law and in the process to wield substantial power.

Plying a time-honored route to legal stardom—through the revolving door of government service—Pogue moved to the vortex of aviation rulemaking, the Civil Aeronautics Board, starting out as assistant general counsel and rising, five years later, to the chairmanship. A diligent, hard-working commissioner, Pogue was respected by the colorful entrepreneurs who founded and ran the airlines and who spent much of their time battling each other and the CAB over routes and rates.

With his intimate knowledge of the Board's byzantine procedures, Pogue was in unique position to represent the carriers when he left the CAB in 1946 to launch his own law firm, Pogue & Neal. To no one's surprise, the airlines followed right behind, blessing the new firm with considerable business from the day it opened its doors. Early clients included Eastern Airlines, which pumped millions into Pogue & Neal's coffers and reigned for years as the firm's largest client.

Possessed now of partnership, power, wealth, the farm boy turned aviation lawyer was nevertheless unwilling to rest on his laurels. Concerned that his boutique practice—top-heavy as it was with aviation work—was too dependent on the airline business, Pogue sought to merge with a more diversified firm, one that would expand his practice base and provide a surer footing for continued expansion. So when he learned that Cleveland-based Jones, Day was discreetly seeking to fuse a local D.C. firm into its then anemic Washington practice, he proposed a union, of sorts, with Pogue & Neal. With the Clevelanders receptive to the idea, a deal was struck providing for the marriage, or reasonable facsimile thereof, of the two firms.

From Pogue's perspective, Jones, Day was the ideal merger mate for three reasons:

- A well-established Cleveland firm tracing its lineage to 1893, JD embodied the wholesome midwestern values Pogue had retained throughout his years in flamboyant, "deal 'em under the table" D.C. A gentleman lawyer with great pride in his profession, Pogue felt a cultural kinship with the Jones, Day partners. They practiced law the way he did. The right way.

- With a broad-based corporate practice, rich in some of the heartland's most prominent banks and smokestackers (including Cleveland Trust, Diamond Shamrock, Eaton Corp., Republic Steel, Sherwin Williams, and General Motors), Jones, Day would add considerable depth to Pogue & Neal's practice.

- Welch's son, Richard Pogue, was a rising antitrust star in Jones, Day's Cleveland office. In effect, the merger would unite two generations of Pogue barristers.

With both sides convinced they were getting the better of the deal, the parties put their names to pen and paper on July 1, 1967, thus linking the two firms. But through the haze of champagne bubbles, all were blinded to a flaw that would wreck the merger little more than a decade later.

The problem was in the stubborn pride and personal jealousies the partners brought to the deal and the role these emotions played in the operating agreements. Although combined as one firm in the merger documents, the practice was nevertheless operated as two quasi-autonomous outposts with different names—Jones, Day, Cockley & Reavis in Cleveland (the home office); Reavis, Pogue, Neal & Rose in D.C.—different bank accounts, and different autocrats in the managing partners' offices, Welch Pogue in Washington and Jack Reavis in Cleveland. While Reavis, head of the much larger entity, considered himself the supreme muckety muck of the merged entity—and the final authority on controversial issues—neither side believed a show of force would ever be necessary. Whatever the documents said, the unwritten understanding between the two gentlemen lawyers was that they would run their respective shops pretty much as they saw fit, except that Cleveland would be responsible for strategic planning (whatever that might be).

"Jack Reavis and my father had a lot in common," says Dick

Pogue. "They were the same age, were both from Nebraska, and they shared a common view of the law and the legal profession. What's more, they were good friends—friends who believed their personal ties would supersede any management technicalities built into the law firm's partnership agreements. They would relate, they agreed, more on the basis of the respect they had for each than on merger documents."

At first, the system met the acid test of a successful merger: the combined entity exceeded the sum of its parts. With Cleveland able to service its big financial and industrial clients through a substantial Washington practice, the volume of business flowed to the nation's capital almost faster than the firm could handle it. Reavis, one of the early architects of a national practice, carefully cultivated the cross-selling potential of his multioffice network. With each outpost feeding work to the other—and with clients drawn into an interrelated web of legal services—the firm began to generate enormous internal growth. To enhance this, the Washington office was sprinkled with a hand-picked group of lateral transfers, each with a highly marketable practice specialty. The most successful, government contracts attorney Eldon Crowell (recruited from the D.C. firm of Sellers, Conner & Cuneo), built so successful a practice that he soon rivaled, some say surpassed, Pogue as D.C.'s chief rainmaker. Just the kind of rivalry that boosts law firm profitability.

From virtually every standpoint, the Jones, Day–Pogue & Neal merger—an early test of the national law firm concept—proved a terrific success, soaring from 83 lawyers in 1967 to 191 ten years later. Everyone was delighted.

Until the "show of force" became necessary.

The trouble started when the home office—dominated by antitrust partners, including new managing partner Allen Holmes* and his protégé Dick Pogue—decided to beef up D.C.'s antitrust capabilities, first by engineering the recruitment of Donald Baker, former head of the Justice Department's antitrust division, and then by ordering Baker to glue on two antitrust laterals to add depth to the department.

While Baker's recruitment raised little ire—a prominent name is always an asset in any practice, especially in statusy Washington— adding two more partners struck many as a bad idea. Antitrust fees

---

*Holmes took over the national managing partnership in December 1974.

barely covered the department's overhead; the newcomers would mean a further drain on the partnership earnings. Although this kind of sacrifice goes hand in hand with practice building—current partners support the new department until it can carry its own weight and ultimately contribute to the bottom line—the sacrifice is generally made in the context of teamwork and cooperation. The partners see the opportunities and draw together to exploit them.

But in this case, the Washington partners at Reavis, Pogue, Neal & Rose believed it was they who were being exploited. Never mind that Welch Pogue (in an apparent peacekeeping move) claimed to be the force behind the antitrust buildup, it was clear even to the most junior associate that Cleveland was calling the shots, forcing the other D.C. partners (who until that point believed they controlled their own destiny) to make a sacrifice against their will. But protest as they did, the additions to Baker's team proved to be a fait accompli. For lawyers raised on the prerogatives of partnership, this was a bitter pill to swallow. Suddenly, they felt voiceless, powerless, manipulated.

"When you work for a corporation, you're an employee of that corporation even if you happen to be the president," says John Macleod, a former Jones, Day Washington partner (assistant to Welch Pogue), now a partner with Washington's Crowell & Moring. "But in a partnership, all of the partners—regardless of their management rank or seniority—consider themselves to be owners, and as such to have a voice in how the firm should be run. Underestimating just how seriously they take this can be a grave mistake."

The battle over the lateral recruits proved to be just the opening salvo. A more divisive battle erupted when Pogue, then in his late seventies, announced his choice for a successor, as Washington managing partner, naming James Lynn over the popular favorite and lead D.C. rainmaker Eldon Crowell. Lynn, who had served as a Cleveland partner before leaving the firm to join the Nixon Administration (he became Director of the Office of Management and Budget), had only recently returned to Jones, Day, this time to the Washington office. Owing to his Cleveland ties and his conservative, midwestern style, the partners once again sensed that the strings were being pulled in Ohio.

"Regardless of what anyone said, it was clear to most of us that Lynn was Cleveland's choice and that the partners who would be most affected by his coronation would have no voice in it," says a former

Reavis, Pogue Washington partner who found himself in the thick of the bubbling controversy.

With innuendos buzzing along the Jones, Day grapevine from Lake Erie to Capitol Hill and back again—and with the Washington partners becoming ever more incensed at what they were hearing about the changing of the guard and ever more determined not to let it happen —it became increasingly clear to the Cleveland high command that the D.C. office would not turn its cheek to the Lynn ascension.

Rather than allow the problem to fester—and watch an insurrection unfold before their eyes—they took decisive action. Welch Pogue (reportedly speaking for himself and Holmes) asked Eldon Crowell and a number of important, Washington-based contract lawyers to leave the firm. Clearly, the decision had been made to rid Jones, Day of a hostile faction within its ranks.

When the news of the housecleaning reached the Washington partners, they were shocked and angered. That the same men who had engineered the recruitment of "antitrust overhead" would add insult to injury by following this up with radical surgery on the office's most lucrative practice had all the markings of a cruel joke. One with traumatic implications for the D.C. office.

Determined to save what they believed was strongest about their office—and in the process to avert an impending disaster—a majority of Washington partners voted to dismiss Welch Pogue as managing partner and to replace him with a management committee led by Eldon Crowell.

Although Pogue responded by stepping down, this was hardly a concession of defeat by the home office. Soon after the D.C. management committee took over, Holmes responded with a thunderbolt, making it clear that he would not recognize them and, furthermore, that the entire government contracts department would have to leave the firm. Faced with this edict, Crowell and the group loyal to him, which by now had expanded beyond the contracts department to include about two-thirds of the office's 43 partners, decided to break the umbilical cord and set up a law firm of their own. On June 1, 1979, Crowell & Moring opened its doors and the separation became official. What had been one firm was now two.

In the years since, both firms have fared well, with Crowell & Moring expanding from its base of 53 lawyers to 120 by 1986 and Jones, Day rebuilding its postbreakup practice from 28 lawyers to 116 in the same period. But while the numbers indicate a rough equivalence, Jones, Day has actually achieved a far more significant accomplishment—one that attests to Holmes's vision of a national law practice and his unbending determination to make that vision a reality.

In refusing to recognize the post-Pogue management committee, Holmes was apparently restating—for all those who may have misread the message in the original merger agreement—that Jones, Day was one law firm, to be run ultimately by one national managing partner, whose authority would never be diluted by colleagues or committees or anything even smacking of democracy.

"Democracy is clearly appropriate and most desired in government," Holmes says. "But it has nothing to do with operating a business, be that a professional practice or any other kind."

"You can't run a national firm by committee," says Dick Pogue, Jones, Day's current national partner and a strict constructionist of Holmes's iron-hand philosophy. "The great strength of a national practice—as we perceive it—is to be able to service clients' needs, often with little advance notice, through a network of offices and practice groups. If we allow internal politics, conflicting chains of command, and other trappings of bureaucracy, democracy, or whatever the hell you want to call it to interfere with that, then we can't deliver what we promise. My God, one of the New York firms—I think it was Paul, Weiss—took more than a year to decide on a lease for their own office space. If that's what democracy does, we don't have any place for it in our law firm."

Is this the head of a partnership speaking? Or is Jones, Day the man's personal fiefdom? The answer is a little bit of both. Clearly, Jones, Day is unique among the megafirms in the way it manages its affairs and in the way it has developed a national practice under autocratic leadership. While an attack on democracy by the managing partner would be cause for revolt at Shearman & Sterling, Baker & McKenzie, or any other giant law firm, at Jones, Day nowadays (since the Washington breakup) it stirs nary a yawn. To the firm's management and to most of its partners and associates, autocracy is one of the secrets of its success.

And successful it has been. Critics and admirers alike admit that the modern management chain of Reavis, Holmes, and Pogue has created an exceptional law firm of superior practitioners that has mastered the marketing arts without sacrificing professionalism.

"We're a business, a professional business but a business neverthe less," says Pogue, who is widely rated as a shrewd antitrust attorney, but whose assets do not include a sparkling personality. "Holmes made our people recognize that the firm had to be viewed this way. Some—who found the idea of working for a business anathema—had trouble adapting.

"I understand how they feel. When I came here, there were 53 lawyers. Not only did I know them all by name, but I knew their kids and spouses too. Now I don't even know all the associates.

"But do I pine for the good old days? Of course not. I can't. As I said, this is a business."

Jones, Day, alone among the megafirms, has defied the laws of nature, enhancing its image as a firm devoted to practice quality even as it expanded. Its eclectic mix of modern marketing savvy and old-school attention to professional excellence makes it among the most highly regarded of the giant law firms.

"Jones, Day is the law firm Finley, Kumble wants to be," says a professor at New York University Law School. "Everything Finley does wrong Jones, Day does right."

The contrast is revealing. Both firms have embarked on ambitious expansion programs that have produced far-flung practice networks. But while Finley has leveraged its growth on star rainmakers, Jones, Day has shunned this approach, relying instead on the legal profession's version of the old mousetrap theory: do better work and clients will beat a path to your door. While this is as tired a cliché as you can find, at Jones, Day it is the gospel. The firm consistently hires top lawyers, places them in rigorous training programs, and insists on thorough, absolutely top-notch work—all of which it believes Finley, Kumble fails to do. That's why it pains Pogue like an abscessed wisdom tooth to be compared in any way to "Kumble & Goin."

"Because we've both grown substantially in recent years, to untutored eyes we may seem like similar law firms," says Pogue, a lumbering Ohioan given to clumsy double-knit suits, cheap print shirts, and clashing acetate ties. "But that couldn't be further from the truth. We may be seeking a similar objective—namely the creation of a national practice—but we have widely different notions of how to get there. To even mention our firms in the same breath is—[raises a fist]—is just [grimaces]—hell, I don't care to discuss it any further."

Pogue's short fuse on the subject reveals a deep-seated phobia over the idea that Jones, Day, regardless of its thoughtful approach to national expansion, may be lumped together with the more reckless bunch.

"There's a creeping fear in the managing partner's office that we'll be known as the Finley, Kumble of the midwest," says a Jones, Day Cleveland-based partner. "The guy goes absolutely bazoo when he reads something that even hints of that. In his heart, he'd love to hold a nationally televised press conference explaining to the world why we're as different from Finley, Kumble as rain and pea soup, but the policy here—one he established—is to take the fifth on any press inquiries relating to Finley. The feeling is—and it's hard to argue with—that headlines screaming our name and theirs will only reinforce the word association that occasionally links the two firms."*

The distaste for Finley, Kumble is a product of Jones, Day's breeding. A prominent firm boasting a stable of prestigious clients long before FK was a gleam in Steve Kumble's eye, Jones, Day sees its megafirm competitor as a reckless newcomer seeking growth for growth's sake regardless of its impact on professionalism. While both are active proponents of national practice, Finley, Kumble went this route to seize opportunity; Jones, Day did so, at least in part, to follow its vagabond clients, to implement the Reavis-Holmes theories on client service, and to reduce dependence on a declining market.

Looking over the local landscape, the Jones, Day ruling clique recognized in the early 1970s that Cleveland (aka "the mistake by the lake") would continue to decline from an industrial center to an urban has-been—one clearly on the wrong side of the manufacturing-to-services transition that would reshape American industry. With its premier smokestackers already reeling from foreign competition and with others fleeing to more promising environs, Cleveland appeared more like a black hole than a market capable of sustaining a law firm's

---

*Jones, Day's January 1986 merger with 75-lawyer, Washington, D.C.–based Surrey & Morse did little to dissuade those who do see the firm as "the Finley, Kumble of the midwest." In merging with a large firm known for a markedly different culture—highly democratic and loosely controlled—Jones, Day gave some weight to Steve Kumble's assertion that others do what he does but simply don't get criticized for it.

future growth. Quietly, for fear of offending its lead clients (most of whom were based in and around Cleveland), Jones, Day made the decision to pursue its greatest growth beyond its home turf.

"There was more to this than just adding up the opportunities and deciding there was a greater yield outside of Cleveland," says a law firm consultant familiar with Jones, Day's internal machinations. "For years, the men at the top of the firm had national ambitions for practicing law in major cities much as the Big Eight accounting firms were doing. But to earn the respect of national clients—especially of the big financial institutions that are so important to large law firms—they believed they'd have to shed the image of a Cleveland firm.

"Let's face it, that city's not seen as a breeding ground for world-class lawyers. You know that phrase from the Frank Sinatra song, something like 'if you're good enough to make it in New York, you can make it anywhere.' No one, except maybe the mayor—and I'm not sure even he's that naive—says that about Cleveland.

"From an image standpoint, the city's a liability. And the Jones, Day people knew it. Even today, ask them if they're a Cleveland firm—which they most definitely are because that's still where the power is—and they'll swear up and down that they're not. Why? I'll tell you. Because they don't want that Cleveland badge lighting up like a neon sign when they take a Los Angeles client to lunch on Rodeo Drive."

Jones, Day's push toward national practice began in earnest with the 1973 opening of its Los Angeles outpost. In short order, the experience proved disastrous enough to have sent all but the most determined imperialists back to the shabby safety of downtown Cleveland. But Allen Holmes—a tenacious streetfighter who would retain his post despite paralyzing bouts with the debilitating neurological disease Guillain-Barré syndrome—was the last man to flee from a challenge. Having committed itself to a new market, to its first major expansion beyond the Cleveland-D.C. corridor, Jones, Day, in the person of its managing partner, was determined to make it work.

No doubt Holmes's ego and his reputation were on the line. But there was more at stake. Having nurtured the dream of a national practice, viewing it for years as Jones, Day's ultimate goal, Holmes simply could not allow the LA office to fold. To do so would be to admit defeat—not just for the West Coast office but for the dream itself.

But in going to LA, Jones, Day made two nearly fatal mistakes that threatened to undermine its practice before it had a chance to put down roots. It underestimated the competition from the local power-houses capable of serving major clients and overestimated the fees it would earn from the big Cleveland client TRW, whose increasing activities in the Los Angeles area throughout the 1950s and 1960s precipitated the law firm's migration to the West Coast.

"Although we had designs on Los Angeles for years—thinking it to be an attractive city in which to practice our brand of law—I can't say we'd have gone there when we did it had it not been for TRW's move," says a Jones, Day senior partner who would talk about the episode only if his name was not used. "Because we'd enjoyed a long and harmonious relationship with them and because they'd grown used to having us as their attorneys, they asked if we'd set up a southern California office. While it would have been entirely possible to dispatch Cleveland lawyers to service TRW whenever the need arose, the client made it clear, in just so many words, that they wanted bodies on the scene, around the clock, and in a real office not a hotel room. And they made it equally clear, or so it seemed at the time, that they'd keep us busy with more than enough work to make the move profitable."

But as other law firms have discovered before and after Jones, Day's LA odyssey, an office launched on a client's promise (or apparent promise) is an office soon flirting with disaster. Inevitably, the costs of starting, staffing, and running the office far exceed budget projections, and to rub salt on the wounds, the volume of fees nowhere matches the firm's euphoric expectations. For Jones, Day, the double whammy hit hard.

For one thing, practicing law in Los Angeles proved to be drastically more expensive than in Cleveland. The wide disparity in rents, support staff salaries, business lunches, entertainment, and incidentals rubbed the Ohioans the wrong way and pushed expenses in virtually every category way ahead of budget. To make matters worse, TRW, the would-be patron saint, found, on second thought, that it really didn't have enough work to keep a local law office busy. What had seemed only months before like the start of a glorious new chapter in the Jones, Day story turned overnight into a quagmire.

And TRW wasn't the only disappointment. Bad luck comes in threes, they say, and Jones, Day was in for the full count.

"In going out west, we'd hoped to develop additional business with other aerospace contractors, some of whom were already clients of our Washington office," the Jones, Day partner recalls. "Because we had an in with them, Northrop and Rockwell were considered sure things. The plan was to snare them first and then to gradually expand the aerospace practice, landing a Christmas list of choice clients who we were certain would fall in line behind the big guns.

"But it never happened. Why? Let's just say the business never developed. But if I had to blame it on someone, I'd point to our own Washington contracts lawyers. Rather than cooperating with the California office—rather than subordinating their own interests to those of the firm's—they insisted that the aerospace clients should be serviced from Washington only. Chalk it up to internal politics: one department, somewhat removed from the mainstream of the firm, jealously protecting its turf."

Strike three came with management's nonchalance toward the difficult and demanding process of carving out a niche in an established market already spoken for by dozens of prominent law firms.

"I have to admit that we thought it would be easier to build a practice in Los Angeles than it proved to be," Pogue says. "Because we were successful in our home territory, because we felt culturally equivalent to the local firms that were most prominent in Los Angeles, we believed clients would seek us out—would bring us their business. But we learned the hard way that being a name in one part of the country isn't enough to buy a Coke elsewhere.

"There's no getting around the fact: we were humbled. We learned that in Los Angeles we had to prove ourselves all over again, and we learned that it would take time."

Seven years worth, to be exact. Seven years of red ink, of disappointment, of internal debate, of appeals by some of the increasingly anxious partners to abandon the office—to let the dream die. For seven aching, interminable years, Jones, Day's Los Angeles outpost was a textbook case of the law office that shouldn't be.

"Opening an office to hold a client's hand is the kiss of death for the office and, in many cases, for the client relationship from which it springs," says a consultant specializing in law firm marketing. "There's more evidence supporting this than the theory of relativity. But firms continue to make the same mistake over and over again and will do so ad nauseam.

"Why? Because the whole thing's so damn seductive. Think about it. A fat-cat client—that's good for say $3 million a year—invites the partners out to lunch (a sure sign that something important is up), to announce that the sun belt's beckoning, that the company is moving somewhere cactus grows, and to suggest that the law firm ride off into the horizon with them.

"The carrot? The $3 million, of course, which the client whispers could rise to $5 million what with pending acquisitions and a big public offering on tap. While he doesn't threaten that you'll lose all of this if you don't call the Bekins truck, the message is, nevertheless, quite clear. But just in case the partners missed it, he finds a way to toss out the names of sun belt law firms who everyone knows would love to have the business.

"Bottom line? The firm commits to a branch office two floors down from the client's digs (have to keep up appearances, you know) in some shiny and grossly expensive glass tower connected to a shopping mall with an indoor ice-skating rink smack in the middle of some hot and smoggy city thousands of miles from the main office. Within months, wood veneer is trucked in for the old world library look, the secretaries are hired, the word processors installed, and the partners, earning $350,000 each, are free to perfect the fine art of doodling. Quickly, the firm discovers that there's not much money to be made in holding hands.

"Soon after, the whole thing begins to unravel. The client winds up talking to those other firms anyway, the mergers never fly, the $3 million shrinks to $1 million, and with the new cost center to support, it's all red ink.

"The moral is that you don't open an office in a distant city just to keep a client. Not unless that client is so big that the firm would collapse without it. You open a new office only if you believe you can build a substantial business there either from scratch or through a merger with another law firm. Should either of these options fail, should you find yourself in the wrong city for the wrong reasons— we are, after all, human—my advice is to turn off the lights, cut your losses, and take the first nonstop home."

Although Holmes reportedly got similar advice from concerned partners, Jones, Day wasn't going anywhere. The dream would not be allowed to die.

"In spite of the problems we had in Los Angeles, Holmes never allowed the office to deteriorate,'' Pogue says. ''He wouldn't let it become a second-class operation just because it was losing money. Top lawyers were brought in both from Cleveland and laterally from the Los Angeles area. New types of practice were developed. Marketing programs were put in place. Synergy with other clients around the country was encouraged. No one could miss the message: we were in this for keeps. Holmes was convinced—as am I—that a law firm that does good work, really exceptional work, attracts clients. Sooner or later the quality sells itself.

''Fortunately, it all began to pay off. The persistence. The hard work. Everything came together. Most important, Los Angeles clients that had given us smidgeons of business over the years started turning to us with increasing regularity—using us as their regular counsel. That was what we'd lacked all along. Until that time we'd had spurts of activity but not the kind of strong ongoing relationships that had built the Cleveland practice.

''Then, in late 1979 or early '80, we started developing this kind of business with the addition of such clients as Ciba-Geigy, the Swiss drug company, Tosco Corporation, the oil and gas concern, and AM International, the office equipment manufacturer whose CEO moved the company from Cleveland to Los Angeles in 1980. These relationships gave us the foundation we needed for substantial growth.''

Jones, Day's LA turnaround is remarkable in its lack of a dramatic event or white knight rainmaker (à la Finley Kumble's West Coast pasha Marshall Manley) that can be credited for reversing its fortunes. Patience, professionalism, and quality work—the same formula Ira Millstein is relying on for Weil, Gotshal's telecommunications practice —made it happen. Today, Jones, Day's thriving Los Angeles practice boasts 23 partners, 49 associates, and three offices (downtown LA, Century City, and Orange County) wired into the city's hottest practices: real estate development, financial services, bankruptcy, and bonds.

In part, Jones, Day's gumption in sticking with LA through the lean years is testimony to its management structure. As undisputed ruler and holiest of holy men, the national managing partner* could pursue his dream for a national practice even if his partners were less than unanimous in their support. Had the issue been put to a vote or

---

*Reavis was managing partner when the LA office opened in 1973; Holmes assumed the top spot in December 1974.

had it been decided by a management committee, Jones, Day might have abandoned Los Angeles, if not in the second year, then in the third, fourth, or fifth. But with his unlimited power, the top man could force the issue with apologies to no one.

"To know Holmes is to know that the man was not going to be thrown off course by bellyachers, hand wringers, or worry warts," says a Jones, Day lawyer who had close contact with the national managing partner throughout the early years of the Los Angeles ordeal. "He believed that leadership meant rising above the fears and phobias of those who were weaker than he—who were so nervous and distracted by day-to-day risks that they were unable to plan for something that would bring the firm long-term gains. That he held his ground with no second guessing is testimony to the kind of stuff he is made of."

Jones, Day's ultimate success in Los Angeles made Holmes's position hard to argue with. Once the office shed its losing ways, turning—as the managing partner steadfastly predicted it would—into a healthy profit center, the doubting Thomases in the partnership ranks lost what marginal influence they had in governing the firm. But while management was publicly patting itself on the back, were there doubts behind the closed doors? Did the Los Angeles experience diminish Holmes's appetite for national expansion? Would he, and in turn his heir apparent Dick Pogue, veto similar forays, enlightened as they now were on the difficulties of building business from scratch?

To those who wondered—who questioned management's resolve —the answer, predictably enough, came in the form of action rather than words. Within a year of the LA turnaround, Jones, Day was on the move again, driving south to what would prove to be the site of its greatest success, Dallas, Texas. This time, however, management took a critical precaution before packing its bags: it merged with a strong local firm connected to some of Dallas's premier clients. What you believe about how and why the deal was structured—and why Dallas became the next whistle stop on the Jones, Day express— depends, to a great extent, on who you speak with.

According to Pogue, it all began with a *déjà vu* when another major client, this time Diamond Shamrock, announced it was moving staff and facilities from Cleveland to Dallas and invited Jones, Day to open an office there. The year was 1979, a watershed for the Los Angeles practice, which was just creeping into the black. The prospect of another major expansion, while part of the master plan, called for some thought. On the positive side, Diamond Shamrock, one of the firm's crown jewels (a client since the early 1960s), served as a vital link to the energy business and generated estimated fees of $2 million a year. Also, Holmes was close to Shamrock's management and served on the board of directors. Responding "no" to the oil company's R.S.V.P. might damage the relationship.

"We were inclined to go to Dallas for several reasons," Pogue says, speaking in a flat monotone that can lull listeners into a coma. "Shamrock was one. National Gypsum,* a second major client moving there, was another. When you have two important clients relocating to another city and asking you to join them, there's considerable pressure to do so. What's more, we thought Dallas an excellent place to practice and had considered it as the site of a Jones, Day practice for some time."

Still, no one was calling the movers. That big clients can lead to big disappointments was made all too clear with the TRW fiasco. For a while, the firm waffled.

"About this time, Holmes got to know Trammel Crowe, the big Dallas-based real estate developer," Pogue says. "I'm not sure how they met, but the acquaintanceship proved to be fortuitous for us.

"It seemed that Crowe had been represented for years by a smallish Dallas firm, Myers, Miller, Middleton, Weiner & Warren—I call them the '3 M firm.' As the developer's interests expanded nationally, he began to feel that Myers, Miller was not big or diverse enough to handle his business. Like many entrepreneurs, he outgrew his lawyers.

"With this in mind, he wanted us to meet with the 3 M people to discuss some kind of amalgamation. Were the two firms to combine their resources, he could keep working with the Myers, Miller lawyers—for whom he had great respect—while at the same time utilizing the services of a much broader practice, namely Jones, Day.

"Another thing. To know Trammel is to know that he's a real Dallas booster. He wants his city to have the best of everything, and at the time, it didn't have a national law firm. That was something Mr. Crowe was determined to change, and with our help he did it. Acquiring Myers, Miller, we opened our Dallas practice on January 1, 1981."

---

*No longer a client.

But was the real catalyst for the move Dallas boosting or Crowe boosting? Was Jones, Day invited to town to fill a legal gap or to fill space in Crowe's office towers? According to a senior partner with the Dallas law firm of Jenkens & Gilchrist, the latter is closer to the truth. Calling Crowe a "real salesman," he insists that the developer first lured Diamond Shamrock to Dallas to take space in one of his buildings and then, seeing an opportunity to strike twice, lured the new tenant's law firm as well.

"Pogue may have construed that Crowe wanted him to come to Dallas primarily to be his lawyer," the partner says, "but I think he heard what he wanted to hear. Getting Jones, Day to Dallas had more to do with the real estate business than the practice of law."

Still another version of the coming of Jones, Day, this from a partner at Dallas powerhouse Akin, Gump, Strauss, Hauer & Feld, holds that the boys from Cleveland decided to accept Diamond Shamrock's "come to Dallas" invitation provided they could acquire a local firm that would assure a minimum level of business while at the same time providing the local savvy Jones, Day lacked. Myers, Miller turned out to be the ideal mate and a merger was negotiated. It was then, and only then, that Jones, Day's relationship with Crowe (the "3 M firm's biggest client") began. In effect, Jones, Day acquired Crowe as the prize in the Myers, Miller deal.

Regardless of whose story comes closest to the gospel—or whether the truth is a combination of tales—everyone agrees that Jones, Day has scored a bull's-eye in Dallas. Starting with 33 lawyers (20 from Myers, Miller and a 13-person contingent dispatched from Cleveland), the office has more than tripled in size, growing to 110 lawyers and becoming one of the city's largest practices.

Jones, Day's success is attributable to a convergence of factors— some which it controlled, others which fell into its lap. In the latter column, Diamond Shamrock, the principal catalyst for the move, honored its promise to generate substantial business, reversing the bad fortune that befell the LA office when TRW failed to deliver. But the firm's other premier Dallas client, Trammel Crowe, falls into the half-luck, half-skill category. While it appears that Jones, Day did little more than inherit the billionaire developer when it acquired Myers, Miller, Pogue was savvy enough to enter the market on the shoulders of a well-endowed, locally connected practice.

Perhaps most important—and for this Pogue and his predecessors deserve full credit—the concept and developing structure (offices in Cleveland, D.C., LA) of a national firm brought an added dimension to Jones, Day's Dallas practice, giving Shamrock, Crowe, and other clients the ability to call on a local firm with offices in key commercial and political centers. A decided advantage over most of its Dallas competitors.

Whether Trammel Crowe sought the arrival of a national firm for the prestige it would bring Dallas is debatable, but there was no doubt that a national practice would serve his far-flung interests. In the same vein, the Dallas presence would enhance the interoffice synergy so critical to Jones, Day's success as a national firm. With Crowe on board, the firm moved zealously in the development of its real estate practice, soaring from 2 to 13 real estate lawyers in Los Angeles (thanks, primarily to work on Crowe's LA projects), doubling the Cleveland department, and adding real estate expertise to the D.C. office. In near-perfect harmony, the national practice helped to write the Dallas success story and Dallas, for its part, has added muscle and momentum to the Jones, Day network.

"Jones, Day rode in here as a good firm with good offices in Cleveland and Los Angeles and nothing to get all that excited about," says a partner with Akin, Gump. "But my Lord, much as it sticks in my craw to admit it, they've built on that foundation spectacularly. Pogue has seen to it that the success they've had here has strengthened Los Angeles and Cleveland and wherever else they have offices. The clients flow from one city to the other and back again. It's awesome to behold. They're no longer a string of offices; they're a strong and cohesive force. Not that they've hurt us—we have considerable strengths of our own that no one can match—but some smaller firms are going to get knocked on their fannies."

Surprisingly—for a profession locked in bitter competition—Jones, Day wins high marks from its local rivals, most of whom recognize it as a major player in the Dallas market. Still, there are the inevitable pot shots when a carpetbagger encroaches (and successfully to boot) on another's turf.

"If success is measured purely by the number of lawyers under your roof, then Jones, Day has done well here," says a Jenkens & Gilchrist partner. "But if name recognition is an equal or more important yardstick, then they've failed miserably. Texans don't know who they are. I've seen three or four name recognition studies conducted by market researchers, and they're always at the bottom of the list.

"The fact is, they've never become part of the fabric of the Dallas business community. They have a few good clients, some of them as new to Dallas as Jones, Day, but they're sort of off by themselves working that field for what it's worth. They're no threat to us, nor to the other good local practices, because they're not really Dallas lawyers and the business community knows it."

Whether Jones, Day is now seen as indigenous to Dallas or is viewed as an obedient satellite of the Cleveland headquarters is a matter of debate. While some in the legal community believe the firm has effectively blended itself into the local landscape, others insist that the old "Cleveland" sign still lights up like a neon marquee whenever a Jones, Day lawyer is present. Although Dick Pogue argues till his face turns crimson that the former is true, the fact is that Cleveland, not Dallas, rules the roost, and to many this is the litmus test of a law firm's true identity. When control is in Los Angeles, it is an LA firm; when control is in New York, it is a New York firm; and, as in Jones, Day's case, when control is in Cleveland, it is a Cleveland firm. Just why this is important relates to the very issue of collegiality that virtually all agree is integral to the maintenance of a strong national firm.

"If Mr. Pogue is Jones, Day's absolute ruler and if he holds forth in Cleveland, where does that leave the Dallas partners?" asks a senior partner with a leading Dallas law firm. "Do they have any control over their destiny? I say no. How can they when all of the grand-scale decisions are being made in Ohio?

"Some say you have to respect Jones, Day's totalitarian structure for the simple reason that you can't argue with success. But my question is, how long will they remain successful? How long will it take for the partners to want more than a financial stake in a firm that's supposed to be theirs, body and soul? If history, if human nature are any guides—and unless Pogue can perform miracles they should be—the partners will seek a political stake as well. Perhaps they've been appeased until now, what with the firm's growth and all, but that may soon be a thing of the past. I understand there's been a cauldron of discontentment brewing over there ever since Pogue replaced Clossey with one of his home-office cronies. If ever there was a Cleveland power play, that was it."

The charge refers to Dave Clossey's announcement in March 1985 that he was leaving Jones, Day (where he was Texas regional partner) to set up an investment banking business for Trammel Crowe. A former Cleveland partner—dispatched to Dallas when Jones, Day opened its office there—Clossey ranked high with Pogue and was rumored to be his choice for the critical assignment of opening Jones, Day's New York office, then on the drawing board.* When he left, claiming what was said to be an exceptional opportunity with Crowe, speculation centered on his replacement, with Dallas partners believing the new leader would be plucked from their ranks. But in what some say reveals a lingering concern from the breakup of the old Washington practice, Pogue named Fred Kidder, a senior lawyer in the Cleveland office, to fill Clossey's post.

"A slap in the face is all you could call that," says the Jenkens & Gilchrist Jones, Day watcher. "At least three or four guys in the Dallas office could have stepped into Clossey's shoes like Cinderella fit into the glass slipper, but they were passed over like a bunch of freshmen watching from the sidelines as the football star gets the campus queen.

"I'll admit, we were taken by surprise when they tapped one of the Cleveland bunch to run Dallas. But now that we've had some time to digest this thing—and I might add to pump some scoop from Jones, Day lawyers interviewing in the job market—we can detect a method to their madness. The way we see it, they just wanted to send an unmistakable message—I mean they wanted to skywrite the damn thing—that in spite of Dallas's emergence as a fat-ass contributor to the firm's treasury, power would flow from one source and one source alone. Cleveland."

Confronted with this view of his motives, Pogue, clearly enraged, rejects the Cleveland power-play theory as "certified nonsense" but then goes on, by way of explanation, to support it. Or so it seems.

"Fred Kidder from our Cleveland office is now in charge of Dallas. *I* appointed him because *I* felt the need to have someone in Dallas whose outlook is similar to *mine*. Although Fred's only been with

*With Pogue exploring several options, just how Jones, Day would enter New York was unknown at the time. Ultimately, the firm gained its Manhattan foothold through the merger with Surrey & Morse, which had a small (22 lawyers) office there.

Jones, Day for five years, he's come to us with considerable management experience at his previous firm, Arter & Hadden. That's the kind of experience *I* wanted in that position.

"My choosing Kidder in no way reflected on a lack of talent in Dallas. Just that the office there is only five years old, the partners are young, and they come from a variety of firms. When Kidder retires in three years or so (he's 62 now), I'm certain that Dallas partners will be considered for the job."

Asked if that meant he'd select a Dallas partner on the next go-round, Pogue grew testy.

POGUE: *I* said *I'd* consider a Dallas partner.

Pogue's consistent use of the first person in describing Jones, Day policies underlines his position as the firm's ruling monarch. While on paper operating responsibilities are delegated to five regional partners (responsible for day-to-day operations, including the supervision of facilities, equipment, and nonprofessional personnel) and five practice group partners (responsible for the law practice itself including quality control and business development),* Pogue can, at his discretion, quash these underlings like an irate king sending his court into exile.

"Our concept is that of a strong managing partner," Pogue says, repeating a theme dear to his heart. "Under the terms of our partnership agreement, I have the authority to run the firm. That power is not shared with an executive or a management committee because we don't have either. Instead we have a partnership committee that advises the managing partner on the selection of new partners and partner compensation, and an advisory committee that consults with the national managing partner on all other issues.

"But in the end I make all decisions. Should I disagree with the

---

*Jones, Day's matrix management system is designed, in part, to disperse power from the branch offices to one of the five key practice groups (corporate, litigation, tax, real estate–construction, government regulations) that cut across geography. For example, a Dallas-based corporate securities specialist would report first to the corporate securities head, located in Los Angeles, and ultimately to the corporate group practice chief based in Cleveland.

committees, I can reverse them. And when I do so, there are no appeals."*

Asked about this apparent contempt for democratic procedures, Pogue cranks out a stock answer designed to silence critics in and out of Jones, Day.

"Call it what you will, our system's always worked well for us. Compare what we have to most of the so-called democracies—better yet, measure their growth against ours—and tell me honestly where you'd want to be."

Pogue's point—about as subtle as the slap in the face he allegedly leveled at the Dallas office—is a rehashing of the old "you can't argue with success" theme. And in a sense he is right. Much of Jones, Day's success over the years is due to ballsy buck stopping by the national managing partners. Free to pursue a common dream, the leaders accepted risks that committees (especially committees of lawyers) would have rejected out of hand. Decisive leadership, as Harry Truman so capably proved, gets things done.

"But even Truman had to answer to the voters," says a partner with the highly democratic megafirm Baker & McKenzie, "and knowing they had this check on their President made his power acceptable to them. But a leader whose power is absolute—and worse yet who boasts about this—is bound, sooner or later, to incur the wrath of his constituents. Faced with a lack of control over their lives—or, in the case of lawyers, over their firm and careers—intelligent people will wake up one morning, look in the bathroom mirror, and ask, 'Why? Why does it have to be this way?' When they can find no rational answer, or worse yet when they get no answer at all, they may leave. Without a true stake in the firm, they'll have no reason to stay. Not when they can get equal or better money, plus a voice in management, elsewhere."

Wishful thinking? Perhaps. Certainly Jones, Day's competitors— especially those who've sought national expansion only to find themselves stuck in a holding pattern—would trade their parchments to see the Cleveland giant abandoned by its partners. But their charges, whatever the motive, do raise an interesting issue. Are Jones, Day partners

---

*While technically Pogue can be dismissed by his partners, this would require a two-thirds vote of the advisory committee, the members of which Pogue himself appoints.

really partners? Or are they glorified employees given the title of "partner" and a share of the profits* but denied the all-important partnership prerogative of a vote in the firm's affairs? ("We never vote," Pogue declares, "except for approving my appointees to the advisory committee—and that's more of a confirmation of my actions than a vote.")

Although Pogue bristles at the notion of partners as glorified employees, it appears to be a fitting description. To call a lawyer a partner, only to remind him that the managing partner's decisions are irreversible, makes a mockery of the partnership spirit.

But will this threaten the firm? Will the lack of democratic procedures—and the ill will this may cause—catch up with the firm as new layers of lawyers, some from mergers with loosely managed firms such as Surrey & Morse, come into the fold? As Jones, Day continues to expand its practice (the S & M merger added offices in New York, Paris, London, and Saudi Arabia), two scenarios are possible. In the first, mounting resistance to one-man rule erupts in widespread dissension, leading inevitably to a repeat of the Washington fiasco and ultimately to the demise of national practice Jones, Day style.

"When partners' egos prompt them to seek more power and when equally big egos on the management side try to deny them that power, then something is bound to erupt," says John McLeod, who helped to negotiate the breakup of Jones, Day's Washington office. "It's one of the main reasons partnerships come apart."

Adds Don Baker, who remained with Jones, Day after the D.C. divorce only to wind up leaving on his own:

"I was with Jones, Day before the split-up but chose not to go with Crowell & Moring. I hadn't been with Jones, Day long and the problems there didn't really bother me at first.

"But eventually they did. In time, I found it intolerable to work in a place where you had no real say in how the firm is run. I served on the advisory committee, a group of 14 partners who met with the managing partner four times a year for the alleged purpose of consulting

---

*At Jones, Day, just who earns how much is top secret. But a Jenkens & Gilchrist partner, who claims to have interviewed Jones, Day lawyers on the prowl, says an average partner (nonrainmaker) with five years experience earns $170,000 to $190,000. Pogue, who refuses to cite specific figures, says this range is too low.

with him on the firm's future direction. But it was just window dressing. He didn't really hear you. . . .

"Maybe in the Reavis days, when the managing partner was down the hall from his lawyers, the Jones, Day setup could work. But when the managing partner is in another city, he has the same problem Caesar had."

Certainly Baker's point, which is shared by others, is well taken. But it must be said that in spite of the iron-curtain system in which they work, Jones, Day lawyers appear to be pleased with their station and proud of their firm. Which raises the curtain on scenario two: Soothed by the balm of a generous paycheck, Jones, Day lawyers will simply resign themselves to the managing partner's power and to the truism that "in a partnership, all of the partners are equal but some are more equal than others."

8

Chicken McLaw: The Boys from Chicago

"An organization crawls at the pace of its slowest members."
Robert Cox, chairman, Baker & McKenzie

If Dick Pogue is an autocrat, Bob Cox, Baker & McKenzie's first full-time chief executive, is a diplomat. If Dick Pogue is a man of few words, Bob Cox is a veritable Ed MacMahon. And if Pogue is as funny as a night in Cleveland, Cox is Chicago's Johnny Carson.

Portraits in contrast, to be sure, but the differences extend beyond the personalities of two megafirm leaders to the very organizations they run and the problems that lie before them. While Pogue commands a cocky, headstrong firm, sure of its place in the world and confident of its mission, Cox can only coax a somewhat stubborn firm to adapt to a changing marketplace, a changing profession.

He may find it easier to scale Mount Everest blindfolded. In spite of its awesome growth, Baker & McKenzie remains, in many ways, a curiously old-fashioned law firm. Consider this:

Weeks after Cox takes office in October 1984, a telephone call comes through Baker & McKenzie's home-office switchboard in a dowdy, time-tarnished office building in Chicago's Prudential Center. A matronly operator, earphone clamped to her head, takes the call.

153

OPERATOR: *Good morning*, Baker & McKenzie. (*It is 4:40 P.M.*)

CALLER: Kindly connect me to the partner in charge of media relations.

OPERATOR: What?

CALLER: You didn't hear me?

OPERATOR: I don't understand what you want.

CALLER: Would you kindly put me through to the partner who handles media relations.

OPERATOR: This is Baker & McKenzie, a law firm. Did you want the hospital?

CALLER: What?

OPERATOR: I'm sorry, but we don't have medical relations here.

CALLER: No, no, MEE DEE YAH relations.

OPERATOR: What's that?

CALLER: Press, newspapers, news. Who talks to the press?

OPERATOR: Hold on (*whispers to other operators*)—I can tell you who to write to.

CALLER: Write to! I'm a journalist working on a story. I have no time to write to anyone.

OPERATOR: That's the rule.

CALLER: What's the rule?

OPERATOR: Hold on—(*more whispering*)—you have to write a letter describing who you want to talk to and what you want to talk about. We'll get back to you.

CALLER: But I can't wait for that. Please, put me through to the managing partner's office.

OPERATOR: I can't do that.

CALLER: Just let me leave a message with his secretary.

OPERATOR: Against the rules.

CALLER: Jesus, isn't anyone in charge of press inquiries on a daily basis?

OPERATOR: Hold on—(*whispering again*)—I am.

CALLER: Who is?

OPERATOR: You heard me, I'm in charge. I've told you what you have to do. *Good morning*, sir. (*It is now 4:45 P.M. Hangs up.*)

Wonderful. The nation's largest law firm—a multinational behemoth with almost 800 lawyers in 31 offices and annual revenues exceeding $125 million—turns switchboard operators into front-line press agents. Why?

"We've just never been comfortable with the media," says Cox, a Notre Dame class of '62 corporate attorney whose thinning hair and choir-boy eyes make him look as if he was growing old and young simultaneously. "The culture around here always saw PR as something for department stores and discotheques, not distinguished law firms. The feeling was that if you had to sell your services, maybe they weren't worth buying."

A notion Cox doesn't wholly reject. Chameleon-like (in part because his career has straddled two generations of law firm philosophy), the 48-year-old, 19-year Baker & McKenzie veteran sees merit in both the old and the new. Like many of his peers among the new breed of senior partners, he is respectful of the past but determined not to be imprisoned by it.

"I have to make my partners see that there's more to public relations than simply beating your chest louder than the next guy. It's my job to make them see that you can use the media to explain your philosophy, to make a statement about your firm and your profession and—and—and damn it to set the record straight on some issues."

Well, actually one issue. One chronic, persistent, pain-in-the-ass issue that drives this otherwise witty and amiable man up the proverbial wall. Namely the galling assertion that Baker & McKenzie is not as much a law firm as a franchise—a thinly connected network of independently owned and operated firms.

"The only thing Baker & McKenzie's missing are the golden arches outside the doors," says a litigator with New York's Rosenman Colin Freund Lewis & Cohen. "Add that and presto, you've got McDonald's.

They're about as much one big law firm as the hamburger giant is one big restaurant.''

Oh, the slings and arrows! Never mind that Cox has heard the charge a thousand times, each attack is as painful as the first. Even more so.

''Why do other firms persist in calling us a franchise?'' Cox asks, fully intending to answer his own question. ''Suppose you're a managing partner sitting there with one or two offices to your name and a client asks, 'How come Baker & McKenzie has 31?' You can't say Baker & McKenzie is smarter or better than you so you take the easy way out and say, 'They're just a franchise.' Easy enough. That it happens to be total bullshit doesn't matter to some people. All's fair in love and war.''

Before the rise of the megafirms—and the attendant competition to be the biggest as well as the best—Baker & McKenzie's organizational structure hardly provoked debate among the premier law firms. But with bragging rights now at stake—much as they deny it, virtually all of the megafirms seek the dubious distinction of being the ''biggest''—and with clients increasingly sensitive to referral arrangements for fear of patchy quality from firm to firm, B & M's claim to be number one is fair game for its predators among the major law firms. So you get swipes like this:

''When the partners in Baker & McKenzie's Zurich office snare the biggest Swiss cheese company in the Alps, they all go out and drink hot chocolate together—or whatever the hell the Swiss drink when they're celebrating,'' says a Finley, Kumble partner, who, many would argue, lives in the kind of glass house that doesn't allow such stone throwing. ''But no one's uncorking the Dom Pérignon in Paris. Why? Because the so-called partners in both offices don't share in each others' prosperity. When the Swiss firm—I see all of the Baker & McKenzie offices as separate firms—gets a big client, virtually all of the money from that client is permanently impounded within Switzerland's national borders. The colleagues in Paris, New York, Amsterdam, wherever, aren't cut in on that action. Oh, a pittance gets out for certain shared operating costs but this is used to lubricate the referral mechanism, not to manage a united, worldwide firm.

''Strip away the veneer and you find that the Baker & McKenzie firms have little in common except some shared clients. To me it's the Kentucky Fried Chicken of law.''

Until the rise of Bob Cox, Baker & McKenzie used to take this kind of abuse lying down. Oh, there'd be fuming and seething and screaming behind closed doors but, given the firm's perceived superiority to "department stores and discotheques," little in the way of offensive PR. Bad press, the logic went, comes with the turf. You toss the clippings in the shredder.

"We used to let the other firms define us," Cox says, salting his shrimp salad as he lunches in the Plaza Club, a private eatery 40 stories above Michigan Avenue. "The process worked like this: Our competitors would call us a 'franchise' and the media would pick up on that because it made for a good, gossipy story. Because we failed to refute the charges in print, they'd be accepted as the gospel.*

"Well that's history. While I don't think I'm ready to hire a PR agency,** neither am I inclined to continue turning the other cheek. The plain fact is that the franchise rap is a falsity, a misconception, a [whispers] fucking lie. One I'm obligated to clear up."

It won't be easy. Much as Cox accepts PR as a positive tool—and as much as he relishes the opportunity to clear the air—in a sense the firm's image was shaped a generation before the chairman entered law school in 1959. Like many of the older law firms, Baker & McKenzie is known less for its current exploits than for those of the man who made it famous. If B & M is viewed as a franchise, blame founder Russel Baker. If B & M is viewed as a global giant, a leader in multinational practice, credit the same Russel Baker.

The story goes back to 1925, when Baker, a transplanted New Mexican who'd worked his way through the University of Chicago Law School, decided to start a law firm in his adopted hometown.

"Looking back at that time, the remarkable aspect of that decision is that I never had any contact with lawyers or with law," Baker recalled in a speech to Baker & McKenzie's summer associates in 1978, a year before his death. "There were no lawyers in my family;

---

*Even Baker & McKenzie's PR coups appeared to backfire. When the *Chicago Tribune Magazine* did a piece on local millionaires, the story on B & M founder Russel Baker followed a closeup on Kegham Giragosian, then president of Chicken Unlimited Enterprises, a rising franchise firm. A B & M staffer, filing away the clipping, wrote across the top of the Giragosian piece "The other franchise success story!"

**Cox has since had second thoughts on this, and is now recommending to the partnership that a PR firm be hired to counsel the chairman on publicity issues.

in fact, I had never met or talked to a lawyer. Why or how the idea to become a lawyer became a fixed purpose with me, I am unable to say. But it did.''

Why start his own practice? Why not join one of Chicago's premier law firms, all of which would have welcomed a bright grad from the city's best school? Baker's comments reveal how dramatically professional competition (and accordingly, starting salaries) have increased since he entered the workplace.

"Fifty-three years ago when I started to work, lawyers right out of school attracted very small salaries. Some worked for no salary at all. It was thought that a period of apprenticeship was necessary before they could be trusted to do serious law work. And perhaps that was true. I noted, however, that the period of apprenticeship was often extended for as long as the victim would take it. . . .''

Penniless, with little to go on but country-boy confidence and a willingness to work round the clock, he joined forces with law school colleague Dana Simpson, hung out a shingle (Simpson & Baker), and proceeded to develop a penny ante specialty representing the city's considerable Mexican community in its bouts with local government.

"As a student I had joined the Spanish Club and began getting to know Spanish speaking people,'' Baker recalled in an interview years later. "Chicago at that time had about 100,000. In 1925, we were having border troubles with Mexico. Prejudice against Mexicans was severe. I made contact with the Mexican Consulate General here and began getting from them what they called 'denial of justice' cases—cases decided against Mexican nationals on the basis of prejudice, not on evidence. As a matter of fact, we had a municipal judge here by the name of Green, a roughneck. Judge Green put me in jail for too spirited a defense of a Mexican.

"The pay was extremely poor. They were economic refugees. They didn't have any money. But they needed help and I had time on my hands. So that's where the international flavor of this practice emerged, defending those Mexicans. And that led to civil cases. One of my clients would be hit by an automobile, for example. I learned to try a lawsuit pretty well. You had to be good to get a verdict for a Mexican. And you had to be lucky." (*Chicago Tribune*, January 28, 1973, by Richard Gosswiller.)

Though the work brought little prestige and about as much money, young Baker, still in his twenties, gained a toehold in the kind of practice that first inspired him to start a firm of his own. Ever since setting eyes on Chicago—through the slats in a rumbling rail car that brought him, cold and hungry, from his native New Mexico into the windy city—Baker had been awed by its commercial muscle, its magnetic pull on the cargo ships, freight trains, entrepreneurs, capital, livestock, dry goods, politicians, and power that gravitated to the city. Baker recognized that the strategic location of Chicago, brawny and bustling even then, made it a natural magnet for international commerce and that this would accelerate once the fledgling aviation industry developed dependable long-distance service.

"Despite the isolationism which dominated the thinking of this country in 1925," Baker said in his 1978 speech to B & M summer associates, there was another current of thought, mainly in academic circles, which held that America would inevitably be drawn into a major role in world affairs, including trade and all branches of commerce. . . . As part of this global perspective, the geographers pointed to the location of Chicago, first as a natural center of transportation, and next as being in the very center of a land mass which extends one thousand miles in every direction, within which radius more than one-third of the productive agricultural land in the whole globe was located. It was predicted by these men that food and manufactured products from this huge granary and production source would be needed to feed, finance and industrialize a large part of the world. . . .

"The first airmail route was established that year, with Chicago as a terminus. Even then it was realized that if air transport developed as anticipated, ports of exit on the rim of the continent would eventually become irrelevant. International routes would overfly them and connect Chicago directly with the foreign centers worldwide.

"These and many other interesting facts were endlessly discussed by young people in college and in the law school. The clear message was that something new, something fresh, interesting and important was in a period of gestation for lawyers. I was among those who liked the idea of working in international law."

"He saw Chicago as the center of the world," says Cox, whose affection for the founder is evidenced by his penchant for telling dozens of gushy Rus Baker stories, "with lines from all of the great cities in Europe, Asia, South America, Africa, and Australia connected into it, creating two-way lanes for money and commerce. Moved by this vision, he saw Chicago as an ideal place not just for another law firm, but for one geared to international practice. He regarded existing law firms as parochial—rarely looking beyond their local, much less national borders—and he wanted to offer clients a worldlier option. Baker & McKenzie would be an international law firm.''

The Mexican-American practice, to which Baker gravitated precisely because of its international flavor, provided the foundation—albeit a meager one—for the multinational firm that would emerge over years. From the earliest days, Baker and his associates learned to be multilingual, to accommodate clients' ethnic and cultural traits, and to deal with lawyers outside of the U.S. (in the early cases, with Mexican lawyers representing client interests on the other side of the border). At first, Baker expanded his international practice in piecemeal fashion, taking isolated cases as they came over the transom. But a big change came in 1934, when Baker, who'd earned a reputation for international expertise, was asked to represent Abbott Laboratories around the world, structuring its supply and distribution contracts, negotiating acquisitions, securing patents, and protecting trademarks. The assignment catapulted him into the world arena to which he'd aspired for nearly a decade and convinced him to focus on building the overseas practice. With prominent litigator John McKenzie joining the firm in 1949, Baker was free to roam the world, confident that the home office was in good hands.

Through the early 1950s Baker's client list expanded substantially (coming to include Eli Lilly, G. D. Searle, Wrigley, and Honeywell), as did his ambitions for a truly international firm with business that flowed not only to Chicago but outward as well to a network of offices throughout the world. The first came in Caracas in 1955, followed in rapid progression by Amsterdam and Brussels in 1957, Zurich 1958, São Paulo 1959, Mexico City and London 1961, Frankfurt 1962, Milan, Tokyo, and Toronto 1963, Paris and Manila 1964, Sydney and Madrid 1965, Rio de Janeiro 1967, Rome and Geneva 1968, Hong Kong 1974, Bangkok and Taipei 1977, Bogotá 1979, Singapore 1981, Buenos Aires 1981, Melbourne 1982, and Cairo 1986. While the breadth of the network is impressive (and unparalleled), the most intriguing aspect of the development process is the unusual way Baker pursued it and made it work.

''We said that we would form a law firm that was truly international,'' Baker told his summer associates in 1978, ''in fact, a firm without nationality if that were possible; that we would recruit linguists and men who had been trained in two systems of law. The small amount of international work that we had handled up to that time convinced us that success in that field required dominion of languages and training in the two systems of law that are always involved in an international transaction.''

To cultivate this transnational organization—one that would cut through national borders rather than rest within them, he hoped— Baker assumed the role of worldwide talent scout, identifying promising lawyers around the world and enlisting them as missionaries in the Baker & McKenzie movement. Typically, a prospect recruited from a Swiss firm—where Baker, representing a U.S. client, witnessed his work first hand—would be invited to come to the U.S. for a stint in Chicago before returning to his homeland to open Baker & McKenzie's Swiss office. In a sense, the headquarters office became a permanent training camp where future partners in the worldwide system were indoctrinated in the Baker & McKenzie philosophy, were taught the fundamentals of the American legal system, and were helped to polish their English.

But the U.S. office was more than a school for foreign lawyers. Baker's master plan called for a cross-pollination between the American lawyers and the visitors, whereby all the participants in the melting pot would absorb through cultural osmosis bits and pieces of each others' customs, languages, and legal principles. As all learned more about their colleagues—and ultimately became more like them—the ''law firm without nationality'' would rise from dream to reality.

''Two things distinguish the way our firm was built,'' says Robert Cunningham, a member of Baker & McKenzie's executive committee. ''In most cases, we had locals, not expatriate Americans, running our overseas offices. That's given us local expertise—and more. Because we've also had this homogenizing of partners around the world, some coming here, others going overseas, our people have been able to transcend their local practices. They've participated in an international culture. A culture based on Russel Baker's view of a global law firm.''

But where Baker's disciples see a cohesive worldwide practice, others see a patchwork of independent entities. To some, Baker's practice of importing lawyers, ''brainwashing'' them in the Baker & McKenzie concept, and then cutting them loose to start practices around the world heralded the dawn of the franchise era.

''What does McDonald's do at its Hamburger University?'' asks the Rosenman Colin Freund partner. "They ship in all of their new franchisees from Decatur, Dubuque, and Des Moines, teach them how to serve a Coke, a burger, and an order of fries in 22 seconds (without dripping the ketchup), and then ship them back to Decatur, Dubuque, and Des Moines to sell all of that good, greasy junk food.

"Well, just substitute litigation for lettuce, cheese, pickles, onions, and a sesame seed bun and you've got franchising, the Baker & McKenzie way. No matter how you slice it—no pun intended—the biggest law firm in the world is really the biggest collection of law firms, each pursuing individual rather than institutional goals."

True? False? All of the above? None of the above? With apologies to those who prefer a clean-cut answer, the answer is "Yes, no, and maybe." The fact is, Baker & McKenzie defies a simple description, in part because its founder was driven by conflicting principles.

Consider partner compensation. Baker's dream of an international brotherhood—of the ultimate collegial environment—clashed with his lifelong obsession with personal incentives linked to individual financial rewards.

Under Baker's formula, partners keep roughly 75 percent of their billings, and the balance is allotted to overhead (primarily local operating costs, with a small contribution toward international expenses). So a partner clocking 1,500 billable hours at $200 per, sends invoices for $300,000 and takes home about $225,000. His standard of living depends, as the great guru Baker believed it should, on his own sweat equity. Good old Protestant, arrive-in-a-freight-car logic: bill more, make more.*

But by encouraging this naked individualism, Baker unwittingly created hundreds of personal fiefdoms that separate the partners as much as or perhaps more than the national borders he sought to avoid. To at least some of Baker & McKenzie's lawyers, the order of loyalties is first to oneself, second to one's domestic office, and third to the international partnership. This defies the spirit, if not the substance, of Baker's multinational fraternity.

Never mind all the "hands across the seas" syrup about which

---

*Cox claims that the compensation system has been refined since Baker's original formula was established, with the current formula now reflecting rainmaking, seniority, and local-office leverage as well as hours billed. So a partner billing 1,500 hours could take home considerably more or less than $225,000.

Cox loves to wax poetic, at least some of Baker & McKenzie's partners likely value the international network primarily for its client referral properties. And there is good reason for this. When the system works well, it's like a Swiss watch. Should a Chicago partner land a world-wide trademark case for a midwest-based consumer products giant, pieces of the work may be handled through Baker & McKenzie offices in London, Paris, Sydney, Caracas, and Tokyo. Lawyers along the route profit from the transaction, by increasing their billings and in turn their personal income (Baker's "bill more, earn more" formula).

"The partner responsible for attracting the client also benefits even if he does none of the legal work," Cox says. "While our compensation formula is keyed toward individual billings, it also provides for those partners bringing business into the international practice. They share in the fees their clients generate anywhere and everywhere in the world."

Cox knows what champagne tastes like. When, as a practicing corporate partner, he landed Equator Bank, a Bahamian outfit, the client brought business to Baker & McKenzie offices in Chicago, London, Paris, New York, and Hong Kong. All of which Cox shared in.

This generous fee sharing—which, like an annuity, keeps paying off as long as the client remains with B & M—is at least partly responsible for the embarrassing gap (similar to that at Finley, Kumble) between rainmaker earnings and those of yeoman partners practicing solid law but contributing inconsequentially to the billings sweep-stakes. At Baker & McKenzie, those partners near the base of the pyramid earn less than $75,000; their brethren ("rich relations" might be a better term) at the apex command $700,000.

Fodder for the firm's critics, who seize the earnings disparity as further evidence of the great franchise conspiracy. Some fried-chicken shops, the charge goes, do better than others. Blame it on location, promotion, or level of service—one outlet's a winner, the other's a dog and at franchises each lives (or dies) on its own performance.

How enviable the role of the critic. Finding fault, when that is the intention, is child's play. Double that when the object of criticism is so broad, so far-flung, so successful a target as Baker & McKenzie. But in spite of its apparent flaws, there is more to Baker & McKenzie than meets the eye. Layers of intermingled relationships, many operating beneath the surface, make the firm tick. The critics never bother to look.

While Cox (inheriting Baker's mantle) overplays the international cheerleader role, and while he may overstate his partners' affection for the "global fraternity,"* he is dead right in calling the franchise charges "bullshit." The truth is, Baker & McKenzie is the largest law firm in the world. And it is more than that. It is a multinational octopus with tentacles extending to major business centers across the globe. More than any other megafirm, B & M can offer clients one-stop shopping for worldwide legal needs within the context of a unified, if not uniform, firm.**

That B & M is more the international firm Russel Baker envisioned than the Chicken Delight its critics insist on seeing is evident by the way the place is run:

- Virtually all Baker & McKenzie partners are signatories to an Illinois partnership† which governs, to a substantial degree, their business and professional lives. This defies the classic franchise arrangement—called "federations" by the Big Eight accounting firms—whereby worldwide practice offices are locked into separate and distinct partnership pacts producing a collage of essentially independent firms functioning to all intents and purposes as a professional alliance.

- Baker & McKenzie's key management committees (executive and policy) set firm rules—including administration,

---

*He loves to tell the following story: "When Rus Baker died in Paris during the firm's annual meeting in 1979, his partners—lawyers from countries around the world—felt the loss as if they were one. Instead of having a single person eulogize him, a microphone was left on a podium at the Inter-Continental Hotel. One by one, many of the partners he'd brought to the firm spoke in the most moving terms about what Rus Baker meant to them. Clearly, he made us all feel as if we were part of a very special international community."

**If Baker & McKenzie has an Achilles' heel, it is in the patchy quality of its legal practice. Conversations with lawyers and clients familiar with the firm reveal a lack of consistency in the office network. Says an executive with a leading industrial corporation: "It can be a frustrating firm to work with. They can be so damned good in some locations, like Bogotá—where the staff's really crackerjack—and so sloppy in others, like Manila. Overall they're good, but those weak spots can piss you off."

†Many are also party to local partnerships in their native countries. Cox claims this is done solely to meet practice requirements for the local bars.

budgets, and professional standards—for the global practice. Should the executive committee mandate a change in standards, this would apply equally to partners in New York, Zurich, and Melbourne.

Equally important, partners worldwide share in the management function. The 47-member policy committee draws its members from each of the firm's offices, and the seven-member executive committee culls partners from each region worldwide. The top spot, the executive committee chairmanship (Cox's post), is also open to partners throughout the global practice. (Wulf Doser, a German partner, served from 1978 to 1981.)

■ When the practice in one country loses money, that loss is shared through depletion of the worldwide operating budget, to which all partners contribute. Such was the case in 1982–84, when the San Francisco office dropped more than $1 million in a messy affair attributed to sluggish business conditions and overzealous expansion into 36,000 square feet of prime office space when half as much would have sufficed.

"No one was happy with the experience but no one balked about sharing the expense," Cox says. "Most of us recognize that a true partnership is one in which the participants can lose money, and make it, together."

■ Most important—and most uncharacteristic of a franchise —Baker & McKenzie is a democracy. A town-meeting, show-of-hands, everyone's-vote-counts democracy. On virtually every crucial issue—from the signing of leases (for more than five years or more than $1 million) to the admission of new partners—the way the firm is run is the way the partners want it to be run.*

For all the prestige that goes with his post, Bob Cox, head of Baker & McKenzie, can't as much as lease an additional 1,000 square feet of office space in the firm's Chicago command post for six years unless 50 percent of his partners—partners in Bangkok, Bogotá, Brussels, etc.—give their consent. Whether this is good business or not—whether

---

*Votes required to carry a proposal range from a simple majority to approve bank loans over $1 million to an overwhelming 85 percent to amend the articles of partnership.

this is the kind of management by committee that set out to design a horse and ended up with a camel—is another issue. The question here, whether Baker & McKenzie is or is not a franchise, must be answered in the negative. McDonald's, Kentucky Fried Chicken, 7/11—none of the archetypal franchise systems operate as Thomas Jefferson democracies. They'll no more grant franchisees a voice in management policies than they'll allow customers to step behind the counter and grill up Big Macs. In its own way, Baker & McKenzie does both. It is one firm.

In a sense, the megafirms differ not as much in the way they practice law (the partners are, after all, interchangeable parts that move freely from firm to firm without adjusting their professional skills) as in the way they are glued together. At Baker & McKenzie, democracy is the prime bonding agent. More than a management structure or a cultural trademark, democracy gives the firm's partners (regardless of their national origin) a feeling of equality, of camaraderie, and of control over their personal and professional destinies. Were this to suddenly change (hypothetical headline in the *American Lawyer*: COX IN BLOODLESS COUP DECLARES HIMSELF KING), were all power to shift to Chicago, the firm would likely collapse within a year.* Under a Dick Pogue–like I-make-all-the-decisions regime, the local practices would soon be competing with the head office, and with each other, for power, control, clients, money. Resentful of U.S. domination, they would likely secede from the Illinois partnership, turning instead to alternate affiliations around the world.

Precisely because it cuts through a complex grid of nationalities, cultures, and languages, Baker & McKenzie, more than any other law firm, must rule by consensus rather than decree.

No one knows this better than Bob Cox. His position, impressive and powerful though it sounds, carries about as much raw clout as the vice presidency of the United States. His effectiveness is measured

---

*The one serious rift in the firm's partnership—the 1971 exodus of much of its Manhattan office—was due primarily to disenchantment on the part of most of the New York partners who believed they were denied a voice in the Baker-dominated management. Some believe this precipitated the move toward democratization. (Incidentally the rebellion, which young Cox, then only in his fourth year with the firm, refused to join, left him as one of only two corporate partners in the office. "Hell, it was lonely there," he jokes.)

not by his ability to seize control, but instead by his success in convincing the partners that control remains with them. Asked for a copy of the firm's organization chart, he presents the graphic on page 168, showing "the partnership," rather than the chairman or the executive committee, at the top.

"My job is not as much to command as to communicate," Cox says, looking, in his conservatively cut black wool suit and starched white collar, more like a man of the cloth than a fearsome commander. "And I've got to find innovative ways to accomplish that. Once a law firm spills over onto a second floor—once the partners can't pass each other on the way to the elevator—they have to find creative ways to relate, to speak, to share ideas. The bigger you get, the more critical that becomes.

"On a recent trip, I visited our offices in London, France, Switzerland, Germany, and Holland. My purpose? To tell them how I planned to run the firm? Not at all. I was there to solicit their concerns, their ideas on what we are as a firm and what we should become in the years ahead. Are there practices or locations that we're in but shouldn't be in? Are there places we're not in and should be? I question, I listen, I learn—and I take all of this invaluable input back to the executive committee, using it as the basis for our ultimate recommendations to the partnership."

In his travels Cox, imitating role model Rus Baker, turns his ear to the associates as well as the partners.

"When I was a partner in the New York office, Baker would stroll in unannounced and ask, 'Wobert,'—always with the Wo—'who are your brightest young associates?' I'd sit down with him, talk about some of the talented young people in the office, and then he'd go off to chat with them alone. Because they represented the future of the firm, he wanted to know that we were grooming the right people and grooming them well. And he was interested in what they thought— in their goals, concerns, and aspirations.

"By the same token, when I travel around the world, I listen as well as talk. I ask my partners, and the associates,* what they have to say. Fortunately, they're not bashful about speaking their minds.

---

*As chairman elect, Cox was dispatched to the West Coast in 1984 to help quell a minirebellion by the firm's San Francisco associates, who believed they were being ignored by management.

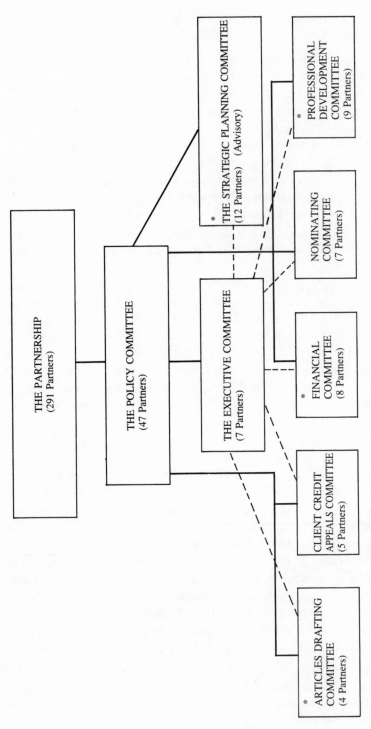

THE PARTNERSHIP
(291 Partners)

THE POLICY COMMITTEE
(47 Partners)

THE EXECUTIVE COMMITTEE
(7 Partners)

THE STRATEGIC PLANNING COMMITTEE   (Advisory)
(12 Partners)

*

NOMINATING
COMMITTEE
(7 Partners)

FINANCIAL
COMMITTEE
(8 Partners)

*

PROFESSIONAL
DEVELOPMENT
COMMITTEE
(9 Partners)

*

CLIENT CREDIT
APPEALS COMMITTEE
(5 Partners)

ARTICLES DRAFTING
COMMITTEE
(4 Partners)

*

NOTE: – – – denotes liaison performed by member of executive committee.
          *   denotes member of executive committee serves as chairman of subcommittee.

Not at any of the offices. The only difference is in the way they express themselves. Some serve you tea, easing gently into the business at hand; others kick your ass the minute you walk through the door. Either way is fine with me because it's their firm and I'm in town to learn how they want it run.''

No doubt Cox could run the General Assembly. A born diplomat, he has an innate ability to balance disparate factions, to form coalitions and, most critical for Baker & McKenzie at this delicate juncture in its history, to lead without getting pushy about it.

"This firm has moved from its first stage, the founder era, to an emerging period of professional management,'' says Dennis Meyer, a Baker & McKenzie Washington, D.C.–based tax partner and former chairman of the executive committee (1975–78). "You have to anticipate some adjustment as leadership moves from something that the founder automatically exercised by dint of his position to something an elected individual has to establish. That's a real challenge, but one Bob Cox is up to.''

Adds another long-time B & M partner:

"The first, last, and only real leader this firm's ever had—to this date, I should add—is the man who fathered it. Because he created the Baker & McKenzie concept and because he was an electrifying son-of-a-bitch, Rus was able to lead by example when he wanted to and with brute power when he chose that route. Remember, he'd built the place and controlled the major clients. He was never much of an administrator, but when you have that kind of buckshot in your rifle, you don't have to be.

"Bob Cox assumes the leadership role minus the client control and minus the deep respect that's paid to the founder. So Bob's role is infinitely more difficult. He can't pretend to be Russel Baker, because he's not, and he can't pretend to have unlimited authority, because he doesn't. He's a fine, highly regarded partner who happens to be facing the greatest challenge of his career.''

Namely, to fill the power vacuum left by Baker's death* and to provide the firm with the kind of full-time professional management a complex, worldwide business needs if it is to remain a vital and growing enterprise. As much as Cox paints himself as little more than

---

*Some say the vacuum was created in the midseventies, about five years before Baker's death, when the patriarch began to ease off from active management.

a global messenger boy linking the partnership to the executive committee, his hope, it appears, is to lead as influentially and effectively as Baker. Driven by an abiding love for the firm, he dreams of shaping the modern Baker & McKenzie to his own vision, bringing to it a new sophistication in promotion (relieving switchboard operators of their publicity duties), finance, and marketing.

In many ways, Cox's challenge reflects the plight of a megafirm struggling to meet the demands of a changing marketplace. In his 1925 dream of a law firm without national borders, Russel Baker failed to anticipate the 1985 realities of volatile currency rates, cash flow crises, market research surveys, Common Market agreements, and coordinated publicity campaigns that require the attention of strong central management. The new chairman's job is to update Baker's original concept to reflect these new and complex demands—and to do so without alienating his partners.

Cox's commitment to the task, a formidable one by any standard, is evidenced by the risk he has assumed in accepting it. One of the firm's better-paid practitioners* (earning an estimated $300,000-plus) at the time he was elected chairman, Cox has subsequently relinquished his clients and with them his long-term financial security. As the firm's first full-time chairman, he is also the first Baker & McKenzie partner to depend completely on the largess of his fellow partners and to risk his livelihood on their support. It is a significant gamble. At a point in his career when a prominent partner is insulated from financial and political risk by his client relationships, Cox is exposing himself to the vicissitudes of a firm that has been devoid of strong leadership for years and that has never before supported such nonproductive (in terms of billings) overhead in the body of a single partner.

Cox accepted the risk, in part, because he longed to return to the management ranks after getting his first taste in lower capacities.

"I served first on the policy committee," Cox reminisces. "Then the nominating committee asked me to serve on the executive committee. I agreed, was elected, and served from 1976 to 1980.

"Looking back, I think I accepted these posts for ego reasons. You know: Robert Cox, executive committee, Baker & McKenzie. Has a nice ring. But once I started serving, I found I thoroughly enjoyed it —to the point that when my last term was over in 1980, I missed it

---

*Although not a barn-burning rainmaker.

terribly. I'd joined this firm because of its international scope—something you experience most in management. So when the partnership recognized the need for a full-time chairman, I was delighted to accept.''

Under the terms of his agreement with the firm, Cox's compensation as chairman of the executive committee equals the average earnings of the 40 highest-paid partners (currently about $400,000). The formula, recommended by Cox himself, reflects his sensitivity to the leadership issue. Being the highest-paid partner (which it is not certain he could have successfully bargained for anyway) might have fueled speculation that he was playing for power, thus defeating his diplomatic offensive in its tracks. Accepting a more modest income, on the other hand, might have diminished the chairman's prestige, making it even more difficult to establish his post as a position of respect.

Certainly Cox's compensation as Baker & McKenzie's chairman does not constitute hardship. The real risk to his personal finances, as well as his professional career, comes at the conclusion of his five-year term. Should his stewardship prove enormously popular—should he accomplish a sweeping modernization of the firm's management practices and in the process propel it to record profits—the partners will surely reelect (at that stage reanoint) their new messiah, or at the very least present him with a rich lifetime annuity. But should he become embroiled in the byzantine politics that run through this mini UN, he may find himself, at age 52, with no clients, no constituents, and nowhere to turn but to the early retirement option built into the chairman's contract.*

In relinquishing his former power base, his clients, Cox has taken a risk rejected by many of his peers among megafirm leaders—those who cling to their clients because they recognize that in the legal community, reputations are made in the practice of law.

''Would anyone even know who Joe Flom is if he'd served his career as Skadden, Arps's chief administrator?'' asks a Weil, Gotshal partner. ''Quite the contrary. No matter how skilled he'd been in that capacity, many in the firm would have viewed him as a wimp who couldn't cut it in the real world—where the money's made.

---

*Cox's plight will be eased somewhat by three years of reentry income guaranteed by the firm should he resume his practice. But he will still have to rebuild his client base to take him into the fourth year and beyond.

"To me, the best analogy is the way a lot of men view their wives. If she's a model mother, lover, homemaker, friend, alter ego, she's still number two because she's not bringing home the bacon. Lawyers, chauvinists that we are, tend to view things this way."

Yes, they do. This partner's boss, Weil, Gotshal's numero uno Ira Millstein, draws much of his mystique, his power, from his reputation as an extraordinary practitioner and unrivaled rainmaker. Ditto for Jones, Day's Dick Pogue.

"I still represent my clients," Pogue says. "They expect it and so do my partners. I think it's vital to my credibility as head of the firm."

On this subject, the usually genial Cox gets a bit cranky.

MARK STEVENS: You're not practicing as a lawyer now but Rus Baker was when he ran the firm. Doesn't that diminish your credibility?

ROBERT COX: I bring certain skills to this job that the firm needs and appreciates.

MS: But you're not practicing as a lawyer.

RC: Hell I'm not. It's just that my firm, rather than outsiders, are my clients.

"The acid test for a law firm leader—the one he must pass if he's to gain his partners' respect—is whether he gives to the firm vastly more than he takes out," says a partner with Los Angeles's O'Melveny & Myers. "If he does, he can have the cherry on top of the cake. Not another hand will reach for it. But if he's seen as taking more than he's giving, forget the cherry—every crumb will be resented. He'll keep his job only as long as he can fight for it."

Cox's quandary precisely. The most significant endeavor of his career hinges on his ability to prove his worth to the worldwide partnership. Worth measured not in measurable billings or the delivery of premier clients, but in the intangible—and for Baker & McKenzie, unfamiliar—quality of full-time management. Is he up to the task? One would have to say yes. The man's personality, his drive, his commitment to the firm should convince the sceptics that this is not a "wimp" seeking to while away his days as a well-paid drain on the partnership earnings. In time it should also be clear that Cox, like

Baker before him, has a vision that is essential to the firm's future performance. A vision of a multinational law firm run as a multinational business, complete with sophisticated financial management (he has since hired a former Arthur Andersen partner to serve as chief financial officer) and, much like a corporate client, with a CEO at the helm.

"Does the same kind of management that worked well for a 150-to-200-lawyer firm necessarily work just as well for a 700-lawyer firm?" Cox asks rhetorically. "I don't think so.

"We may have an anomaly here, in that a partnership, which is generally thought of as professionals working together, has to pay for its success in the form of centralized management. Maybe there comes a point, in sheer size, where that becomes essential."

As risky as his role may be, Cox is clearly on to something. As one of the first to recognize (or at least one of the first to admit) the need for a lawyer–chief executive devoted exclusively to running his firm, he is likely to emerge in years to come as a pioneer in legal management. With the megafirms continuing their explosive growth from once-clubby professional practices to complex commercial entities, the tradition of part-time management will go the way of the detachable shirt collar. Insisting that management is somehow demeaning, somehow a lesser form of achievement than the practice of law, is a macho conceit that will have to be abandoned if the firms are to successfully balance growth, quality, and profitability.

"Imagine a Fortune 500 corporation expecting its president, who rose through the sales ranks, to spend half his time calling on distributors," says a Baker & McKenzie partner and strong Cox supporter. "That would be absurd. It's comforting to know that your CEO has experience in the field but you don't want him making a sales pitch in rural Minnesota when he should be concerned with broader issues. If the chief executive's focus—in a corporation or a law firm—is split between personal and institutional interests, he won't be effective. Given the best of intentions, he can't be. In spite of his title, he's only human."

No megafirm challenges this ban against dual interests to a greater extent than Chicago's other legal giant, Sidley & Austin. At S & A, chairman Howard Trienens divides his time, titles, and offices between the law firm and its biggest client, AT&T. In dual roles that appear almost schizoid, he is both Sidley & Austin's unchallenged leader and senior vice president, general counsel, and head of the legal staff for the huge telephone company. An unusual arrangement in this day and age, but one that dates back to the firm's beginnings as the attorneys that incorporated Western Electric Manufacturing in 1872.

Ever since Alexander Graham Bell's famous message, "Mr. Watson, come here, I want you," carried almost miraculously through the first rudimentary telephone, the law firm that would become the modern Sidley & Austin has been inexorably linked to the communications empire that sprang from Bell's invention. As early as 1881, Sidley predecessors—the Chicago firm of Williams & Thompson, which had represented Western Electric—drew up the corporation charter for Chicago Telephone, one of the first Bell subsidiaries. At that time, the firm's name partners, Messrs. Williams and Thompson, became major investors in the new venture.*

Blessed with a growing reputation in the still fledgling telephone industry, the firm gained important new clients stemming from another dramatic invention of the times: Thomas Edison's incandescent lamps. In 1882, the firm handled the incorporation of Western Edison Light Company and performed similar services for Chicago Edison. Along with telephone and electric, the firm built practices representing railroad clients (including the Atchison, Topeka and Santa Fe) and local probate cases. As a young and ambitious America began to flex its commercial muscle, the law firm found itself wired into the dynamic service industries that would fuel the nation's growth.

Over the years, these early specialties (with the exception of electric utilities) remained the bedrock of Sidley & Austin's** practice, with the telephone business commanding the greatest share of the firm's resources and providing the greatest single source of its fees. This reached a crescendo about a century after Bell's first patent was issued, when Sidley was called on to represent AT&T in a tangle of antitrust suits brought by competitors seeking to make headway in the long-distance business. Later, S & A counseled Bell in the intricate divestiture of its operating companies.

---

*The initial capitalization called for 5,000 shares at $100 each.

**Partner William P. Sidley's name was reflected in the firm's name by the turn of the century; Edwin C. Austin was so honored in 1937, when the firm became known as Sidley, McPherson, Austin & Burgess. Then in 1967, after several intermediate names, the name was changed again to the current Sidley & Austin.

As a prominent antitrust lawyer whose career has reflected Sidley & Austin's familial relationship with the phone company ("I've worked on phone company matters since joining the firm in 1949") and as S & A's chairman, Howard Trienens found himself in the thick of the legal fireworks. With legal matters dominating the phone company's affairs—and with their outcome destined to play a critical role in the onetime monopoly's ultimate fate (as would later be the case with Union Carbide)—AT&T's newly elected CEO Charles Brown wanted his old friend and trusted adviser Howard Trienens at his side. In September of 1979, S & A's top partner was asked to join the phone company as the head of its sprawling (then 900 lawyers) and somewhat shell-shocked legal department. Making it clear that he would not leave Sidley ("after 30 years with the firm, there was a way of life I didn't want to change"), Trienens accepted Brown's offer, provided he could remain chairman of the law firm. Determined to have him at virtually any cost, Brown agreed.

On January 1, 1980, Trienens took up his AT&T post, where he continues to serve. Shuttling weekly between New York (where he plays corporate executive) and Chicago (where he holds forth as law firm chairman), Trienens balances his seemingly incongruous roles as head of one organization and the employee of another. But does he balance them? As a key authority on the selection of outside law firms and as the head of the firm that is selected most often, is he not in position to reward his partners at the corporation's expense?

"I bend over backwards to see to it that other firms get work from us," Trienens says as he eats a sumptuous luncheon in AT&T's elegant private dining room atop its vault-like office tower on New York's Madison Avenue. "The last thing I want to do is run up Sidley & Austin's share of this corporation's legal bills. This client doesn't want to be dependent on a single law firm, and the law firm doesn't want to rely on a dominant client."

Wait a minute. With the law firm chairman considered so indispensable that he runs the client's law department and with Sidley claiming roughly half of AT&T's outside legal fees (about $12 million), is there not dependency? And what of the fact that the phone company's billings account for about 20 percent of Sidley's fees?

"What of it is right," Trienens says. "You can read anything you want into it, but in fact it's just a good relationship with a client that goes back to the time when Bell acquired Western Electric and got the law firm (we'd been representing Western Electric since its founding) along with the purchase.

"I came here not for personal advancement—I don't see this as the crowning achievement of my career—but instead to satisfy a client's request. And we've built in certain checks to rule out even the appearance of conflicts.

"First, all of the staff lawyers here with the authority to hire outside counsel can select the firms they think best suited for any matter before them. Sure, they may want to run the choice by me, but the decision's theirs to make. And they, nor I, choose only Sidley & Austin. In the course of my work here, I've called on Dickstein, Shapiro & Morin; Davis Polk; Paul, Weiss; Dewey, Ballantine—all for work that Sidley & Austin could have done but for which I didn't choose them. Contrary to the popular perception, the relationship between Sidley & Austin and AT&T is unlike that between IBM and Cravath. We don't tell Sidley to handle one area of practice, like litigation, and then have the law department handle all the rest. Instead, in-house lawyers and various outside law firms are mingled together on a wide range of cases and projects.

"Second, I don't pass on any of the bills from Sidley & Austin. They go directly to Mr. Brown.

"And third, I'm not compensated by Sidley & Austin for my work with AT&T. When the partnership shares are calculated, my contribution here is not counted. For that reason, although I'm chairman, I'm not the highest-paid partner in the firm. And I can't personally enrich myself by building Sidley's share of the client's fees."

Still, checks and balances notwithstanding, one keeps coming back to the undeniable fact that there is an apparent conflict here—one only a Solomon reincarnate could master while keeping the client, the law firm, and his own professionalism intact. Which makes it all the more astounding that Trienens appears to pull it off. As much a target as a turkey on Thanksgiving, he manages to avoid the barbs of hungry competitors, all of whom would give their eye teeth for even a modest helping of Ma Bell's fees, and to retain the loyalty, if not reverence, of his Sidley & Austin partners.

"In general, I don't like the idea of a law firm partner heading up a law department," says General Foods' Peter DeLuca. "I don't even like it when there's a partner on the board. It limits the corporation's ability to decide between law firms for any given matter.

"This much said, if anyone can strike this delicate balance, it's Howard. He's unique. And he has a special, unusually warm relationship with Charlie Brown. If he's not Charlie's closest confidant, he's one of them."

Adds a senior megafirm partner who has observed Trienens ("sometimes eyeball to eyeball across the table") for more than 20 years:

"Watch a pro golfer drive his ball down the fairway. It's deep, it's straight, and most incredible to a duffer like myself, it's effortless. There's no groaning or grunting or wasted motion. And that's exactly the way Howard Trienens practices law and manages his law firm. The guy's got so much on his plate that most lawyers—and I think I'd have to include myself in that category—would choke trying to digest it all. But he makes it look easy. He's a superb lawyer who's always thoroughly prepared, and judging from the success of his firm, he's a darn good administrator too. Sometimes you just have to recognize excellence, and I think just about everyone in this profession will agree that's a fitting description of Howard Trienens."

Sitting with the man, you have to scratch your head to believe this is what all the fuss is about. Dressed in a dreary gray worsted suit that threatens to overpower his gangly physique, he exudes none of the high-voltage ego of an Ira Millstein or the tough-guy vibes of a Dick Pogue. In a courtroom, he'd be taken more for a bailiff than the world-class attorney who holds the AT&T account in his hip pocket. But behind the gaunt face and balding pate of this 62-year-old former Air Force lieutenant there is, by all accounts, a natural leader who in spite of his part-time management controls the firm and shapes it—with counsel from the executive and management committees—in his own vision.

In a sense, his leadership is a hybrid of Dick Pogue's and fellow Chicagoan Bob Cox's. Like Pogue's, his decisions are not subject to a firmwide vote. But where Pogue functions as a lone ranger, Trienens works within the executive committee, seeking a consensus among the other firm leaders (including Blair White, Eden Martin, and Newton Minow) and the partnership ranks in general.

"I can never allow myself to get too far ahead of the partners," Trienens says. "Should I awake one morning with the idea that we should have a Miami office, I can't just go out and open one the following week. I'd have to determine that I'd have support on that. If it didn't make sense to the partners, we just wouldn't go."

What Trienens omits from this humble assessment of his powers is that his sponsorship of a Miami office would be reason enough for most of the partners to support the move. Would Bob Cox love that! While Baker & McKenzie's newly installed chairman must rule by consensus—while he must count heads before proceeding with any major action—Trienens leads more by influence than electioneering. Like Cox's larger-than-life predecessor Russel Baker, Trienens commands respect for what he is rather than for the powers he draws from the organization chart.

That he has dual responsibilities has not hurt the firm. Since 1980, S & A has experienced dramatic growth, claiming the number five spot among all law firms. And beyond the numbers, Sidley has managed to develop an international practice (offices in Los Angeles, Washington, D.C., London, Singapore, Cairo, Oman, and Dubai) without being labeled a franchise. No mean feat in a jealous, catty profession that would love to lump the two Chicago megafirms together.

Conclusions? That a full-time chairman is unnecessary? That law firm leadership is best dividing its time between internal management and client service? Perhaps, when the leader is a time-honored link to the firm's glorious past and a present-day bridge to its richest client. But short of that, the choice is not so clear. Sidley's Eden Martin, widely regarded as among the new generation of firm leaders, puts it this way: "Howard will be succeeded one day, but he'll never be replaced."

Adds a prominent legal consultant:

"In the big firms today, there are no easy answers."

Epilogue

Just how the megafirms will fare in the future is open to debate. While optimists foresee an ever expanding market producing unrelenting growth, with the firms crossing the 1,000-lawyer mark in the early 1990s, those with a darker view predict, as they say on Wall Street, a "correction" that will find many of the giants with more partners and associates than there are clients to keep them busy.

What management sees in its crystal ball determines, to a great extent, how it prepares for the future. But because all the firms are dealing with hunches, guesswork, and old-fashioned intuition, even the most careful planning may do little to assure success. Managing partners will likely face the same predicament as the senior partner at a major New York law firm who was asked by the Manhattan Chamber of Commerce to address its membership.

Accepting months in advance, he forgets about the engagement until, cleaning off his desk late one Friday evening, he notices the date scheduled in his calendar for the following Monday. With a big weekend at the beach house on tap, there's no time to write a speech.

Instead, he calls in a bright young associate.

PARTNER: Smith, I have to address the Chamber on Monday night and because of a client commitment all weekend, I can't

do it myself. You'll have to write it for me. Have it on
my desk by noon Monday.

ASSOCIATE: But sir, my girlfriend and I have reservations at—

PARTNER: On my desk at noon. No ifs, ands, or buts.

Comes Monday at 12, the speech is delivered, freshly typed and bound
in a neat plastic folder. The partner, on his way to a client meeting
that will last until the evening, stuffs the speech in his briefcase without
reading it. Later that night, standing before the audience of 500 business executives (many clients and potential clients), he delivers the
speech, which turns out to be a literary pearl filled with humorous
anecdotes, wonderful insights, and bright observations on the law,
business, and modern society. Near the end, it reaches a crescendo
that has the audience on the edge of its seats.

"Before I leave you tonight," the partner reads, "I want to share
with you my ultimate vision for using the law not only to resolve
disputes, but to create a new chapter in the history of mankind. A
chapter of unparalleled peace and prosperity worldwide. To accomplish
this, I will suggest that we"—he turns the page, curious himself to
read this remarkable plan, only to find, in capital letters, IMPROVISE,
YOU SON OF A BITCH.

Index

181